Praise for
Comfort When the Shadow Falls

"In the thirty years I have known Eddie Sharp, he has served the church with skill, integrity, and steadiness. This book is a treasure for all who seek to do the same. Thank you, Eddie, for this great book and your decades of faithful service."

—**Max Lucado,** pastor and best-selling author

"A cogent reflection is the powerful thesis of this book: 'The broken-hearted need shoulders, not sermons.' Join a caring, seasoned minister, who offers biblical grounding, personal wrestling matches with mortality, grief dynamics of the dying, families, and communities, and especially the sacredness ministers have in journeying with, rather than 'fixing,' grievers. Eddie's shared personal narrative, formed by a lifetime of learning by being present, is truly a gift to all."

—**Virgil Fry,** Executive Director, Lifeline Chaplaincy

"I know of no one more qualified to write this book than Eddie Sharp. I've seen him walk everything he talks in these pages. He brings experience, compassion, and wisdom to this critical conversation. But most of all, Eddie's thoughts on death and grief replace simplistic platitudes with a gospel big enough to embrace pain, mystery, and hope. Read and be blessed."

—**Rick Atchley,** Senior Teaching Minister, The Hills Church

"*Comfort When the Shadow Falls* gently, kindly, generously inspires and teaches us that we can each be used by God as he fulfills his promise to bless those who mourn. This excellent resource blends Scripture, human behavior, and practical advice. It feels like being mentored by someone with decades of experience carrying 'the presence of Jesus into any and every situation—standing and not running away.'"

—**Jan Taylor,** Director of Corporate Communication, UK HealthCare, University of Kentucky

"A thoughtful and well-written guide, deeply grounded in both truth and compassion. I have not discovered a more helpful, comprehensive resource in thirty years of oncology care. This excellent book should be in the library of all ministers and any other follower of Christ involved in a ministry of comfort."

—**Jacqueline Matar,** MD, radiation oncologist, Lexington, KY

"This is a thorough discussion of life and death and a deep and perceptive delving into the full meaning of God's intention of life for his children. A clear presentation of the full scope of the Gospel for our daily lives of our experience with the deaths of those we love. A helpful description of the comfort we can know when the shadow falls."

—**Will Norton Jr.,** Dean of the School of Journalism and New Media, University of Mississippi

"Having been on the receiving end of a caring, thoughtful, and present minister during the illnesses, deaths, and funerals of my husband and mother, I know first-hand the value of having a minister's involvement to provide critical support throughout the journey of loss and sorrow. This book offers concrete, detailed, and compassionate advice that can help any pastor better meet the needs of her or his congregation as members encounter unavoidable end-of-life experiences."

—**Anne Ray Streeter,** PhD, former Associate Professor of Communication, Lindsey Wilson College

"As a journalist, I often encounter religious leaders in the midst of tragedy. Many times, these ministers and other caring people of faith are thrust into a heart-wrenching situation—be it a natural or man-made disaster or a fatal diagnosis—with little training on how to serve the dying and grieving. That's what makes *Comfort When the Shadow Falls* so important. Its compelling mix of real-life anecdotes, helpful Scriptures, and sensible advice is much needed."

—**Bobby Ross Jr.,** Chief Correspondent, *The Christian Chronicle*

COMFORT
WHEN THE
SHADOW FALLS

COMFORT
WHEN THE
SHADOW FALLS

ENCOURAGING THE DYING AND
THOSE AFFECTED BY GRIEF

EDDIE SHARP
in collaboration with CHERYL MANN BACON

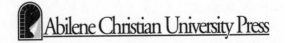

COMFORT WHEN THE SHADOW FALLS
Encouraging the Dying and Those Affected by Grief

Copyright © 2019 by Eddie Sharp and Cheryl Mann Bacon

ISBN 978-1-68426-230-4 | LCCN 2018039910

Printed in the United States of America

Scripture quotations, unless otherwise noted, are from The Holy Bible, New International Version®, NIV®. Copyright © 1973, 1978, 1984, 2011 by Biblica, Inc.® Used by permission. All rights reserved worldwide.

Scripture quotations noted NRSV are taken from the New Revised Standard Version Bible, copyright © 1989, the Division of Christian Education of the National Council of the Churches of Christ in the United States of America. Used by permission. All rights reserved.

LIBRARY OF CONGRESS CATALOGING-IN-PUBLICATION DATA
Names: Sharp, Eddie Leon, Jr., author.
Title: Comfort when the shadow falls : encouraging the dying and those
    affected by grief / Eddie Sharp, in collaboration with Cheryl Mann Bacon.
Description: Abilene : Abilene Christian University Press, 2019.
Identifiers: LCCN 2018039910 | ISBN 9781684262304 (pbk.)
Subjects: LCSH: Church work with the terminally ill. | Death—Religious
    aspects—Christianity. | Grief—Religious aspects—Christianity. |
    Bereavement—Religious aspects—Christianity. | Funeral rites and ceremonies.
Classification: LCC BV4338 .S53 2019 | DDC 259/.4175—dc23
LC record available at https://lccn.loc.gov/ 20180

Cover design by Gore Studio, Inc. | Bruce Gore
Interior text design by Sandy Armstrong, Strong Design

For information contact:
Abilene Christian University Press
ACU Box 29138
Abilene, Texas 79699

1-877-816-4455 | www.acupressbooks.com

19 20 21 22 23 24 / 7 6 5 4 3 2 1

Acknowledgments

This book is a labor of loving intimidation. Over the years of my ministry, I have been blessed to be able to serve hundreds of families in times of sickness, injury, death, and grief. My ministry has not been all dark times, but I have walked with many on very cloudy days. Along the way, dear ones have suggested that I write a book, sharing my experience and practice of ministry in times of loss. I never minded sharing these thoughts with classes of ministry students at Abilene Christian University, but I was not eager to write a book about them.

One of those urging me to write a book was Dr. Cheryl Mann Bacon, my dear friend, who was the chair of the Department of Journalism and Mass Communication at Abilene Christian University and a member of University Church of Christ, where I was senior minister for twenty-eight years. Cheryl was delightfully persistent until 2016, when she turned to being *persistently* persistent. She secured a sabbatical for the spring semester of 2017 for the express purpose of editing this book, which she was sure I should write. Jason Fikes, the director of ACU Press, agreed to receive the manuscript when complete to see if it would be valuable to others.

So we began. I wrote chapters on my personal journey with mortality and my ministry with those needing comfort. Cheryl was the editor of the book and added two chapters of her own from her areas of expertise, writing obituaries and news coverage about death. And here we are, years later, with a finished book. We hope it blesses our readers so that they can bless others.

I want to thank Cheryl for her energy and vision, which got us to this point. She is thoughtful about language and form in communication. She is just as thoughtful about the hearts of those around her. Working with her was a constant delight.

I want to acknowledge and honor my father and mother, Leon and Billie Sharp, and Cheryl's mother, Betty Mann, who died while we were writing this book. We were writing about loss as we were losing those dear to us. This book is not theory; it is real life and authentic practice.

I want to thank Gray and LeeAnn Thornton for letting me use their house on Lake LBJ as a Sabbath place to write without interruption while surrounded with nature's peace and beauty.

I want to thank the churches in Texas, New Mexico, and Nevada who let me minister with them over the past forty-seven years. I especially appreciate the leaders and members of University Avenue Church of Christ in Austin, who graciously allowed me the time to write and considered it ministry to the greater Body of Christ in the world.

Finally, I thank my wife, Annette. She has supported and encouraged me along the way. She has taught me much as she has bravely and faithfully faced her own severe bouts with breast cancer. She has been my minister and has led us into greater spiritual transformation. She has been and is gracious out of the very heart of Jesus. I dedicate this book to her.

Contents

Preface.. 13

1 A Gift from Scripture: Faithful Reflection and Hope 15

2 The Heart of the Minister in the Shadow of Death.......................... 27

3 Ministry to the One Dying.. 43

4 Ministry to the Family of the One Dying 59

5 The Place of the Funeral in the Ministry of Comfort........................ 71

6 Funeral Customs and Rituals... 81

7 Serving the Unchurched with the Love of Jesus 93

8 Obituaries as Ministry and History 101

9 When Death Is News... 113

10 Through the Shadows to the Light:
   Extended Pastoral Ministry to the Grieving.............................. 123

11 The Church of Sorrows and Acquainted with Grief........................ 135

Preface

Our desire for this book on ministry in times of death, dying, and grief is to give hope to those who are called to minister in these times. The call to ministry in the name of Jesus holds many delights. Joys of new life and new light encourage us as disciples. The harder moments of ministry take us into the colder shadows of life. The real world calls for some faithful men and women to serve the dying and the grieving—without hiding places or excuses. Perhaps together we can learn how to survive the discomforts of the ministry of comfort.

A Gift from Scripture: Faithful Reflection and Hope

I have often told people that ministry feels like living in a lightning and thunder world. Lightning strikes at someone else's house, and the thunder shakes where I live. If you are a minister or a committed Christian with a gift of caring in crisis, you know what it means when the phone rings, bringing the thunder of another's loss into your life.

The paradox of ministry is unrelenting. Jesus came to give life, but had to die to deliver it. The blessed peacemaker must walk into conflict. Those of us who are called to minister comfort to others must enter discomforted rooms of tears, loss, anger, stunned silence, and numbing ache. The gift God wants to give through us must be given in the places where it's needed—no matter how messy or difficult.

We live in a world where people too often need the ministry of comfort. The gift of life carries within it the mar of mortality. Death is everywhere.

Through his ministering servants, the ministry of comfort puts skin on the love and presence of God. Being in the right place, keeping silent vigil, or sharing caring words helps keep the trial of loss from becoming an occasion of hopeless despair.

Scripture gives us an unfolding story of the nature of death and the possibility of any hope in the presence of death. The ministry of comfort as we understand it now has its roots in the way the biblical witness reveals what life and death are and what God is willing to do for men and women facing mortal realities. The Old and New Testaments reveal the development of faithful reflection and hope in the face of death.

Old Testament Views of Life and Death

Adam and Eve, our old relatives, stepped out of the garden of life into a world of sweat and thorns that would be both birthplace and graveyard for all their children. Sin brought a mortal world; life would have an end. Even given how long those first generations lived, a day came for each person that was their last day, last light, last breath. Even Methuselah, who lived 969 years, knew his time was coming.

In the early chapters of Genesis, death makes itself known—in Abel's murder, in generations of natural mortal comings and goings, in the flood judgment of God. God's promises to Abraham grow out of Abraham's faithful life and arc into a future beyond his death when he will be gathered to his people and revered as the father of the faithful. Still, Father Abraham knew the finality of death. He reminded God in Genesis 15 that if God was going to be faithful to his word, he would have to bring Abraham a son from Sarah before they died. Otherwise, his chief servant, Eliezer of Damascus, stood to receive all of Abraham's earthly estate. The lifespan of Abraham set a defining boundary for the work of God.

Isaac was finally born when Abraham was a hundred years old and Sarah was ninety.

So it is for all of us. What God will do with us eternally begins with what God will do with us in this breath-boundaried life. And what the evil one hurls against us to thwart the plans of God will be worked out in the same time frame. The evil one uses the fact and fear of mortality as one of his primary tools when he attempts to distract and discourage people on their pilgrimages from cradle to grave.

The Old Testament gives us a wonderful unfolding of hope in the face of death. Three texts in particular highlight the development of expectations of life: Psalm 6:5, Job 14, and Isaiah 26.

"Among the dead no one proclaims your name. Who praises you from the grave?" (Ps. 6:5). This text represents a host of references to those who are dead and in the grave (Hebrew: *Sheol*), where the dead rest in a realm of darkness away from life and the face of God.

In Psalm 88, the distress of the psalmist is as deep as death itself. We hear the psalmist's understanding of the nature of death from this cry for God's attention:

> LORD, you are the God who saves me;
>> day and night I cry out to you.
> May my prayer come before you;
>> turn your ear to my cry.
> I am overwhelmed with troubles
>> and my life draws near to death.
> I am counted among those who go down to the pit;
>> I am like one without strength.
> I am set apart with the dead,
>> like the slain who lie in the grave,
> whom you remember no more,

who are cut off from your care.
You have put me in the lowest pit,
in the darkest depths. (Ps. 88:1–6)

Death and the pit of the dead hold no hope in this psalm. Yet those who love God hope against the pit. Job whispers such a hope:

Mortals, born of woman,
are of few days and full of trouble.
They spring up like flowers and wither away;
like fleeting shadows, they do not endure.
Do you fix your eye on them?
Will you bring them before you for judgment?
Who can bring what is pure from the impure?
No one!
A person's days are determined;
you have decreed the number of his months
and have set limits he cannot exceed.
So look away from him and let him alone,
till he has put in his time like a hired laborer.
At least there is hope for a tree:
If it is cut down, it will sprout again,
and its new shoots will not fail.
Its roots may grow old in the ground
and its stump die in the soil,
yet at the scent of water it will bud
and put forth shoots like a plant.
But a man dies and is laid low;
he breathes his last and is no more.
As the water of a lake dries up
or a riverbed becomes parched and dry,
so he lies down and does not rise;
till the heavens are no more, people will not awake

or be roused from their sleep.
If only you would hide me in the grave
    and conceal me till your anger has passed!
If only you would set me a time
    and then remember me!
If someone dies, will they live again?
    All the days of my hard service
    I will wait for my renewal to come.
You will call and I will answer you;
    you will long for the creature your hands have made.
(Job 14:1–15)

Job expresses a rather fatalistic view of the human condition: we are a miserable lot, assigned to live out our days like hired laborers, dying like withering flowers, "so he lies down and does not rise."

But Job has a thought that gives him hope. "What if we could be like trees instead of flowers? Trees can appear dead and done, yet sprout anew out of freshly watered roots. What if God could hide the dead with his hand and then remember them? If God could remember them, he could bring them life."

Whether God will allow the dead to live again seems to hang on God's longing for reunion with those who have lived faithfully before him. Will he call their names? Job believes the voice of God could call back the dead. This is not a well-developed doctrine of death and life after death, but in the chasm, we can hear a faint echo of hope.

Isaiah also brings a message of greater hope when he writes to call God's people to faithfulness. For those who choose to follow the living God instead of dead idols, Isaiah writes of a hope beyond the blessings of this life:

They are now dead, they live no more;
    their spirits do not rise.

You punished them and brought them to ruin;
>   you wiped out all memory of them. (Isa. 26:14)

But your dead will live, LORD;
>   their bodies will rise—
let those who dwell in the dust
>   wake up and shout for joy—
your dew is like the dew of the morning;
>   the earth will give birth to her dead. (Isa. 26:19)

Certainly, God will bring judgment on those who persist in their rebellion and sin. Generations of God's forbearance will end with destruction and captivity for the sinful. But even as the assurance of the wrath of God rings out, hope can be heard. While the enemies of the Lord face certain and complete death, the people of God anticipate life, even liberation from the grave. They will stand, shaking off the grave's dust.

One Old Testament story illustrates the ability of God to bring back his faithful ones from the realm of the dead. In 1 Samuel 28, Saul consults the witch at Endor, seeking to visit with dead Samuel. God allows Samuel to come back from death to deliver the prophecy of Saul's soon and certain demise. Samuel had died, but he was still Samuel. He was a faithful follower of God even as one sent back from the dead.

The intimations of hope in the Old Testament, when taken together, make a compelling argument that God intended from the beginning to give his faithful ones the blessing of resurrection from among the dead.

The Promise of Life in the Ministry of Jesus

The promises of life everlasting in the Old Testament prepare us for the good news in Jesus Christ. Jesus does not see death as an insurmountable situation. He confronts death in his ministry work. Jesus walks into the house of Jairus and raises his daughter from the dead (Luke 8:40–56). Jesus meets a funeral procession outside of Nain in Galilee. He raises the young man from the dead and gives him back to his mother (Luke 7:11–17). Jesus has dear friends in Bethany (John 11:1–44). One of them, Lazarus, dies. When Jesus gets to Bethany, he comforts Mary and Martha, telling Martha, "I am the resurrection and the life. The one who believes in me will live, even though they die; and whoever lives by believing in me will never die. Do you believe this?" (25–26). Then Jesus calls Lazarus out of the tomb into the light of resurrected life. These accounts of Jesus raising people from the dead establish clearly that the power of God can overwhelm death. Life in God is stronger than death in the world.

Jesus also confronts death and affirms life in his teaching ministry. In the last week of his ministry, Jesus lectures the Sadducees on eternal life (Luke 20:27–38). The Sadducees did not believe in the resurrection of the dead. They only believed in the first five books of the Old Testament, in which they found no indication of a promise of resurrection. They asked Jesus a complicated question that grew out of a hypothetical situation in which a woman had a series of seven husbands who all died. The Sadducees asked: "At the resurrection, whose wife will she be?" Jesus replies that in the afterlife, there is no marrying or being given in marriage. People in the afterlife are like angels. They are God's children because they are the children of the resurrection (35–36). Jesus goes on to counter the Sadducees' denial of the resurrection using the call of Moses in Exodus. Moses calls God the God of Abraham, the God of Isaac, and the God of Jacob. Then Jesus says of God, "He is not the God of the dead, but of the living, for to him all are alive" (38).

This teaching should encourage all who read it. God intends life for his children.

The Impact of the Death and Resurrection of Jesus

The teaching of Jesus during his ministry does encourage us to believe that God's power overwhelms death. The miracles and the teaching set the stage for what could not have been imagined. What was not clear during his ministry, and what could not be clear until his resurrection, was the place of the resurrection of Jesus in the demonstration of God's power to give life to his children. Our hope in the face of death rests in the death and resurrection of Jesus, not in the words of Moses or in the reemergence of Lazarus. The death, burial, and resurrection of Jesus is the core of the good news of the Christian faith that Paul shared with the church at Corinth:

> Now, brothers and sisters, I want to remind you of the gospel I preached to you, which you received and on which you have taken your stand. By this gospel you are saved, if you hold firmly to the word I preached to you. Otherwise, you have believed in vain.
>
> For what I received I passed on to you as of first importance: that Christ died for our sins according to the Scriptures, that he was buried, that he was raised on the third day according to the Scriptures, and that he appeared to Cephas, and then to the Twelve. After that, he appeared to more than five hundred of the brothers and sisters at the same time, most of whom are still living, though some have fallen asleep. Then he appeared to James, then to all the apostles, and last of all he appeared to me also, as to one abnormally born. (1 Cor. 15:1–8)

Paul had opposed the followers of Jesus, but that opposition died the moment he realized Jesus lived (Acts 9:4–6). For Paul, the resurrection made following Jesus make sense.

Without resurrection, following Christ is foolishness. Living like we have hope if the world is actually hopeless is just pitiful (1 Cor. 15:18–19). But living in hope does make sense because the resurrection of Jesus has been verified by eyewitnesses. "But Christ has indeed been raised from the dead, the firstfruits of those who have fallen asleep" (1 Cor. 15:20).

The resurrection of Jesus topples the specter of death from its ominous throne. The evil one has used the imminence of death to hold all in the vise grip of fear. In resurrection, the power of God defeats death through Jesus:

"Where, O death, is your victory?
Where, O death, is your sting?"
The sting of death is sin, and the power of sin is the law.
But thanks be to God! He gives us the victory through
our Lord Jesus Christ. (1 Cor. 15:55–57)

The incarnation of Jesus joins God with our human condition. The writer of Hebrews makes it clear that mortals had been held in bondage not by the power of death, but by the fear of death:

Since the children have flesh and blood, he too shared
in their humanity so that by his death he might break
the power of him who holds the power of death—that is,
the devil—and free those who all their lives were held in
slavery by their fear of death. (Heb. 2:14–15)

In Jesus, eternal God knows the heartbeat of our mortality through the Word that became flesh. Jesus breaks the power of Satan and liberates all who come to him from the prison that is the fear of death. Because of that freedom, the Christian's life becomes life eternal. Thus, having an indestructible life, and with courage in the face of death, the Christian may freely follow Jesus into the ministry of the cross.

We follow the example of Paul, who, compelled by the love of Christ, lived his life leaning into the resurrection hope:

> I want to know Christ—yes, to know the power of
> his resurrection and participation in his sufferings,
> becoming like him in his death, and so, somehow,
> attaining to the resurrection from the dead. (Phil. 3:10–11)

Biblical teaching stands over against the understandings of death and the afterlife in the first century AD and in our time. In my master's thesis, I explored the belief in natural immortality versus a reliance on the resurrection power of God. While there may be some sense of an immortal essence in a person, the clear biblical teaching is that our hope for the future depends on the power of God and not on our own natural possession of an immortal soul. Oscar Cullmann compared the death of Socrates with the death of Jesus in his book *Immortality of the Soul or Resurrection of the Dead? The Witness of the New Testament.*[1] Plato, who writes about the death of Socrates in *Phaedo*, described the death of Socrates as a sober, deliberate act. Socrates drank the hemlock, then had his friends touch his body, beginning at his extremities. He talked about how the body was the prison house of the soul as he noted the creeping numbness moving toward his heart and head. His calm reception of his death was a model for others to follow who believed this expression of Plato's cyclical view of time and his belief in the immortal human soul.

In Platonic philosophy, nothing was final about any one life or death because the one dying would be reborn from the unseen world into the seen and then back to the unseen to start over again. Plato believed that a person was a soul that had a body. The aim was to purify the soul through multiple lifetimes. Ultimately, the soul would be released from the wheel of time and allowed to merge into some kind of world soul—the Ideal Person.

Cullmann contrasted the death of Socrates with the death of Jesus. Jesus sees death as a real enemy. Jesus prays with great passion in the garden that the cup of the cross might not be his. Jesus expressed the desolation of dying in his "My God, my God. Why have you forsaken me?" Jesus shows no hint of the detachment of Socrates. For Jesus, his one life mattered.

The Christian view of personhood and time is not cyclical; it is linear. The Christian view of our person is of a body–soul unity. The writer of Hebrews expresses the significance of our one and only life: "Just as people are destined to die once, and after that to face judgment, so Christ was sacrificed once to take away the sins of many; and he will appear a second time, not to bear sin, but to bring salvation to those who are waiting for him" (Heb. 9:27–28). We are born. Our lives begin. We each live our one and only life. Our choices make all the difference in the eternal outcome of our lives. What we do with the invitation of Jesus to find life in him makes all the difference. Without Jesus, we have no promise of a good outcome for our immortal soul. Life eternal and everlasting hangs on our faith in Jesus and the power that raised him from the dead working to raise us.

In our ministry to the dying and the bereaved, we maintain a more Christian stance as we express our hope in terms of resurrection rather than innate immortality. We believe that in Christ, immortality is inaugurated in us—we have become immortal through Christ. The presence of the Holy Spirit is the presence of our eternal life already resident in us. All hope for life after death depends on the work of God.

The Christian Hope and the Heart of the Minister

Resurrection faith generates resurrection hope, leading to acts of love undergirded by the resurrection power of Jesus:

> I pray that the eyes of your heart may be enlightened
> in order that you may know the hope to which he
> has called you, the riches of his glorious inheritance
> in his holy people, and his incomparably great power
> for us who believe. That power is the same as the
> mighty strength he exerted when he raised Christ
> from the dead and seated him at his right hand in the
> heavenly realms, far above all rule and authority, power
> and dominion, and every name that is invoked, not
> only in the present age but also in the one to come.
> (Eph. 1:18–21)

As ministers responding to the lightning and thunder of ministry, we do so in the strength of the risen Christ. As ministers of God's comfort, we also rest in the hope offered in Jesus. Hope in Christ soothes our own fear of death. Whatever ministry gifts we have in our public roles of preaching or teaching in the kingdom, we want to distinguish ourselves even more in the private, hidden moments when the face of death glares at us and the work of death mocks us. As we move into this book, we will maintain a constant connection with the hope that is in Jesus Christ and the teachings in Scripture that comfort and argue eloquently for peace.

Note

[1]Oscar Cullmann, *Immortality of the Soul or Resurrection of the Dead? The Witness of the New Testament* (London: Epworth Press, 1958).

The Heart of the Minister in the Shadow of Death

The fear of death has stalked me since I was a boy.

When I was ten years old, my parents bought the 1960 edition of *Compton's Encyclopedia*. My dad made a deal with me. He would pay me ten dollars for every volume of the encyclopedia that I read. Every now and then, I would start the reading challenge. I never finished the first one, but I know a lot about aardvarks and Alabama. I read about people in the process. I was troubled in reading about John Adams, Archimedes, and almost every other figure in the book—they were almost all dead.

The listing for my friend President Adams was "John Adams, Jr. (1735–1826)." Almost everyone in the book had a year, a dash, and another year listed. At that point, I knew I had my first number, 1951, and I had my dash working. But my dash seemed to be working inexorably toward some distant second number. I remember thinking, "If even the people who make it into the encyclopedia have to have a second number, what hope is there for those of us who will never be famous enough to be mentioned?"

Out of this encounter with mortal reality, I framed the personal statement "I am going to die."

It was a problem. I thought about it in the night. I would suddenly be struck by the stark reality of the statement and would just panic. Once in Carlsbad, New Mexico, on a Sunday evening while my dad was preaching, the cold wind of death suddenly swept over me, and I ran out of the auditorium and kept running in panic until I collapsed. I could not outrun the truth, the fear. Death taunted me as I lay gasping in the grass: "You can run, but you will never, never, never escape."

This chapter provides a glimpse of my personal journey into ministry, especially ministry in times of death and grief—the journey that began when I was ten years old.

Two years later, when I was baptized in 1963 before I turned twelve, I remember thinking that dying might be okay that night. But I was still held in the fear of death. When I watched *Star Trek*, I would think, "By the time anything like this happens, I will have been dead for centuries." The bumper sticker that reads "It's not that life is so short, it's just that you are dead so long," captures in pithy fashion some of the elements of my fear. With a heart so inclined to mortal anxiety, I pursued the study of ultimate reality in physics for a while before turning to the study of the ultimate realities of God and the Bible. I started preaching in 1971 at age nineteen with many loose ends of my life hardly settled—but the tide was turning in the battle with death.

The anchor verse to stabilize my life was in Hebrews:

> Since the children have flesh and blood, he too shared
> in their humanity so that by his death he might break
> the power of him who holds the power of death—that is,
> the devil—and free those who all their lives were held in
> slavery by their fear of death. (Heb. 2:14–15)

I found myself steering into the cold wind of my fears. More and more, I moved toward loss, grief, and death. My inner dread remained, but I opened myself to face and move closer to my fear. My graduate work helped. Studying under Tom Olbricht, J. D. Thomas, Eugene Clevenger, and Everett Ferguson gave my heart constant nurturing from the biblical doctrine of hope and life, leading to a clearer understanding of hope given through the risen Christ and the Holy Spirit. My master's thesis, *The Biblical Doctrine of Life After Death,* forced me to face more directly the central, defining fear and reality of my life. Some nights, my research brought stark moments, and the academic investigation of my topic brought near the existential crisis of my life. I would find myself hurrying out of Abilene Christian University's Brown Library into the night, where I could leave my thoughts behind and reset my heart under the Texas stars. Wrestling with these fears extended the writing of my thesis a full year beyond its allotted five-year term. I tell people that I was finally able to overcome my fear of death when my wife, Annette, told me she would kill me if I didn't get the thesis done.

That disciplined, academic study of death was important in framing my ministry to the dying and their loved ones. I also had the opportunity to face death and its influences in my early ministry. Trent, Texas, is a small place, largely marked by a big truck stop on Interstate 20 west of Abilene. But the tiny community of 330 people and the tinier congregation of sixty-five where I ministered still encountered the same life-altering grief that is synonymous with living and dying anywhere. Preaching there during graduate school provided regular opportunities to sit with families in their grief and to search for the right words for the funerals. I found that being present with the grieving did not demand that I have everything about death and dying in my own life worked out. I could be fearful and faithful at the same time, as long as I was present. And that understanding set a certain direction for my life and ministry.

The people in these places also have lessons for the minister. In Trent, the lessons were often taught by the little widows who took me in and taught me how the potlucks came together for the family and taught me the customs of a little town. In Trent, that meant the people standing around at the graveside stayed and filled in the grave, and so I learned that in these small places, death is something that people participate in. While they were teaching me about funerals in a small town, I also learned the stories of their lives.

Today, many young ministers are serving in young, suburban churches where they may work for several years before they are called upon to minister to a dying person or to that person's family. During the years I was at University Church of Christ in Abilene, where we had a large elderly population, Rick Atchley was across town at a much younger congregation that had very few funerals. The problem with that is if you have a funeral, it's horrible—children born with life-threatening conditions, teenagers killed in car accidents, young parents leaving behind a grieving spouse with young children. In a big, young church, you're going to have very challenging funerals. You're also going to have few people with experience ministering to the dying and grieving. For the young minister then, it's important to seek out those parts of the community that are less sheltered, less young and healthy, where death arrives more frequently or without notice.

In every place I have preached, I have let local funeral directors know that I was available and willing to do funerals for people without churches or connections to ministers. In Albuquerque and Carlsbad, New Mexico, and in Abilene, Texas, I was called upon many times to help such families. Most often those grief circles taught me much about the way pain and loss worked in individuals and in networks of families and friends. I would see the best and the worst in people. I had the opportunity to talk about noble folks and about some who seemed to have completely wasted their gift of life.

I also received some special training in death and loss in critical incident situations. While I was preaching for the University Church of Christ in Albuquerque, I was trained and served as a volunteer chaplain for the Albuquerque Police Department. APD trained its volunteer chaplains to support the first responder corps—APD officers, firefighters, emergency crews, and hospital emergency room personnel. Chaplains also learned how to deliver death notifications to families of victims of auto wrecks, murders, and other tragedies. This training was pivotal in my development as a minister in times of loss. We saw bad things. I delivered bad news. I learned during this phase of my ministry that I wanted to be a minister who could carry the presence of Jesus into any and every situation—standing and not running away.

Breaking the News

I've served as a police chaplain in more than one city, but my training began in Albuquerque, New Mexico, where I was tutored by Jack Price, a chaplain and member of the Albuquerque police force who was so admired that when they built a new police headquarters there, they named it for him.

Training included some classroom time, some one-on-one, then riding along with another chaplain. And finally, we took the calls. Sometimes notifications were made accompanying another police officer, but often I was on my own.

One evening, I received notification there had been a murder at the Blue Goose bar on Central in Albuquerque. I went to the bar and got the address of the deceased from the police officer and left to do the notification.

The simple frame house was in the southeast part of Albuquerque. I climbed the three or four steps to the front porch where the porch light was burning. A small Hispanic woman opened the door.

"I'm Eddie Sharp. I'm the police chaplain," I said.

I had a badge and drove a blue-and-white police cruiser, so when folks answered the door, they knew this stranger did not come bearing good news. When chaplains do a death notification, the first question is, "Is so-and-so home?" It's always important to ask, because at least once the name I'd been given was wrong, and so for that family the angel of death passed over.

But in this case, she answered, "No." He wasn't home.

With the early, simple questions, you're giving a little emotional space to deliver bad news and allow it to be received. Any time I tell bad news—even an announce-ment in the pulpit—I begin gradually. "As you may know, the Johnsons often vacation . . ." Always give that insulation—give people time to catch up emotionally to the fact that there could be bad news coming.

Standing on that front porch, I began those questions.

"Is he out?"

"Yes."

"Did he go out with his brother?"

You want the person to start asking the questions as realization slowly rises.

"Is something wrong? Is he hurt?"

"Yes. Did he ever go to the Blue Goose?"

"Yes. Is it bad?"

"Yes, ma'am. I'm sorry, it is."

"Is he dead?"

"Yes, ma'am."

At this point, the conversation pivoted and she began to cry. I asked her if she had other people at the house and if she needed my help to tell them. She said no, and I stood on the porch and heard four different people begin to cry as she moved through the house and told her family.

Death notifications are hard duty, but they are real, face-to-face ministry. Like a lot of other things in ministry, you have the satisfaction of knowing that you've handled a terrible thing in the best possible way. It drains you, and you have to recoup by returning to life, to your family, to soccer fields and folding laundry, to car pools and mowing the lawn, to places where life happens.

How Spiritual Formation and the Rule of Life Shape Ministry

Developing a responsible ministry to the grieving required more than overcoming childhood fears, adolescent escapism, and the determination of a young adult. Giving attention to personal spiritual formation added an essential, deepened relationship with God. Beginning in 2011, my wife, Annette, and I entered a program of training in spiritual formation with Ruth Haley Barton and the ministry of the Transforming Center in the Chicago area. This journey has allowed me to reframe the early experiences of my life in terms of first-half-of-life growth and development, and it taught me to appreciate who I am now in terms of second-half-of-life blessings and growth. *Falling Upward* by Richard Rohr describes this first half of life to second half of life movement.[1]

Rohr says the first half of life is dominated by the nature of our first self or, more accurately, our false self. Each one of us is born with a certain genetic makeup into an imperfect family structure set in a fallen historical, social context. We develop the personality and interpersonal skills necessary to survive and perhaps flourish as we meet our world defined by our struggles. The fact that we are raised in a Christian home does not change this. We deal with life using our first-self strengths into our thirties and forties. As we enter the second half of life chronologically, we may begin to differentiate ourselves from the circumstances of our early life and live less reactively and more intentionally. Rohr says in the first part of life, we build our house; in the second part of life, we learn how to live in it. You do not arrive in the second half of life; you journey on.

The best way to open oneself to this critical transition is through the disciplines of spiritual formation. In her book *Sacred Rhythms,* Barton explains how the seven spiritual discipline practices contribute to the heart of the minister, preparing them to help those dying or grieving.[2]

The beginning of the journey of spiritual formation is desiring the Spirit of God. The word from Paul is for us to be filled with the Spirit (Eph. 5:18). The imperative sense of that indicates that we have a part in our spiritual—Spiritual—journey. We have to want God. We have to want the fullness of the power of the presence of the indwelling Spirit of God. Jesus asked the two disciples who came to him in John 1, "What do you want?" (John 1:38). Isn't that the question?! What do we want? Are we ready to give up finding our strength and support, even as ministers, in some place other than God and the fullness of his presence? We will certainly read all we can. We will go through various trainings. God will use everything we learn and practice to his purpose and glory. Still, the evil one always tempts us to do godly things out of our own power and resources. Godly things done out of ungodly resources will never bear good fruit. So we begin with desire for God at the center of our lives. When we are facing the most profound moments possible in life, we will need deep resources. We cannot dig our own wells deep enough to deal with death and dying, losing and grieving.

Through the second discipline, solitude, we find a gateway to further spiritual development. Without the capacity to be in solitude, we live our lives in an anchorless, foundationless whirl. The French philosopher Blaise Pascal wrote in his *Pensées*: "All of humanity's problems stem from man's inability to sit quietly in a room alone."

Jesus often goes to the solitary places to be alone. "Very early in the morning, while it was still dark, Jesus got up, left the house and went off to a solitary place, where he prayed" (Mark 1:35). A lonely person is one without other people. A person in solitude is a person alone with God. In solitude, a person can sit with herself—as she is—without the need of others to define or distract her. Ernest Becker, in *The Denial of Death*, wrote that people are often driven into all kinds of negative behavior because they cannot sit alone with their mortality.[3] Other negative thoughts and patterns can drive us to distraction. Recreation, online worlds, even legitimate business can generate the noise necessary to give us a place to hide from our life as it is. The point of practicing solitude is to be with what is in the presence of God. Reflect on that—to be with what is in the presence of God.

Solitude makes a container for silence, the third discipline. I was trained to be a radio disc jockey in the days when we actually had vinyl records to spin on a turntable in a studio. Part of the training to play records, present commercials, and give public service announcements was to be able to play all of this seamlessly, creating a constant flow of noise. The great evil in the Top Forty radio world was silence. Silence was a sign of incompetence. Yet, our spiritual well-being depends on our willingness to be in silence with God. Psalm 46:10 teaches that our mighty God calls for us to take time for silence in his presence: "He says, 'Be still, and know that I am God.'"

Solitude and silence cooperate in us to create space for us to sit with God. The practice of solitude and silence creates in us a place to begin in our daily lives. The practice of solitude and silence becomes a "reset" button for our heart, our emotions, our priorities.

In the presence of dying, death, and grief, having a practice of solitude and silence in the presence of God gives the minister a proper place from which to rise and enter the turbulence in the lives of others. We as ministers need to be able to move from God-filled quiet into the dark chaos. If we ourselves live only in chaos, what gifts will we have to bring to others? Bringing our inner upheaval to others is no gift. It is better to rise from the quiet—from silent communion with God.

Our desire for God's presence in our lives and our lives in God's presence leads us to solitude, silence, and prayer. In solitude and silence, we come to sense the presence of God with us. The discipline of prayer has its beginning when we open our heart to the Father who comes to us. Prayer as communing with God begins wordlessly as the Holy Spirit, no doubt, intercedes for us (Rom. 8:26–27). This may be remarkably different from the way that we started to pray. Most of us began praying by trying to find the right words. Often, people are considered masters of prayer because of the way their words roll out in rich images and mellow tones. In a public worship service, I like to pray with someone who is sensitive to the power of words and tone. As a child, I began my own praying with words. Later, sometimes my lack of prayer was because I did not have the words or did not want to struggle to find the words. Ultimately, my wordy prayers were born from other wordy prayers. Now my worded prayers arise from silence and solitude. Often, my prayers now begin not with a word, but with a posture of leaning my body forward into the presence of God who is with me.

With this form of personal prayer as a foundation, a minister is ready to pray for others. Prayer that begins in solitude and silence will find the right words for those in sorrow. The prayer may have fewer, simpler words, but they will have been formed in the presence of God.

Spiritual formation creates space for us to encounter the presence and holiness of God. The living God comes to us. The triune God—Father, Son, and Spirit—comes to us in various ways. Solitude, silence, and prayer put us in a living, spiritual relationship with God as he is and in our lives as they are. The next move of spiritual formation is to make the way we encounter Scripture a matter of the head, heart, and hands—not just something for our heads. The discipline of *lectio divina,* or holy reading, allows our reading of Scripture to move from our intellect to our emotions and on to our behavior.

Lectio divina may be done individually or in groups. It involves reading a passage of Scripture several times with periods of silence between each reading. The listener is asked to be sensitive for a word, a lesson, or a godly behavior that flows out of the text. The point of the holy reading is to let the Word of God settle deeply into the heart. So much of our Bible study is an intellectual pursuit, as if our lives were transformed by the accumulation of facts. In the same way that solitude, silence, and prayer open us to the presence of God around us, *lectio divina* opens us to the presence and work of God in Scripture.

This way of encountering Scripture shapes the way we use Scripture generally in ministry. Preaching texts should be texts that have been allowed to settle from head to heart in the minister. The way Scripture undergirds the minister's work with the sorrowing matters. Scripture needs to flow from the heart of God into the hearts of the dying and bereaved. The minister's heart is often the link between the heart of God and the hearts of the hurting. Learning to let Scripture speak to our hearts transforms us as ministers, allowing us to be conduits of the truth and compassion of God as God fulfills his promise to bless those who mourn through us.

The sixth of the spiritual formation practices I want to consider is *examen*. With our desire for God leading us to solitude, silence, prayer, and holy reading, we come to the necessity of regular assessment of where we are in our walk with God and regular recommitment to be completely his. *Examen* can take several forms. At its heart is a daily inventory of our lives that asks, "Where today was I walking most closely to God?" and "Where today was I walking at some distance from God's will?" *Examen* leads us to prayers of thanksgiving for the opportunities to live to God's glory. *Examen* leads to what Barton and others have described as gentle noticing of our errant ways during the day. It is not that our bad words, attitudes, and actions are not serious matters; rather, spiritual directors encourage spiritual pilgrims not to give the evil in their lives too much power or notice. So the language used is, "Gently notice your shortcomings, ask God for his forgiveness, and move on with your life."

Our desire to be in a process of being conformed to the image of Jesus for the glory of God, the sake of others, and the blessing of our own lives demands daily attention to the path we are walking. We are thankful for the good steps we take; we are contrite, but hopeful, as we deal with our failures. As ministers who enter the high-pressure environments of death and dying, we cannot possibly speak and act perfectly in every moment. Our faults will become evident under pressure. We practice self-examination so we can begin each day renewed by the continuing grace and mercy found in the blood of Jesus and the sanctifying power of the Holy Spirit.

The seventh discipline is a rule of life. A rule of life is a person's plan for a coherent, consistent commitment to maintaining spiritually transformative practices. This includes daily disciplines, a weekly practice of Sabbath, and plans for other times of retreat during the year. Living perfectly by such a rule of life is impossible, but no significant, long-term journeying in spiritual transformation is possible without the thoughtful formation of one's own rule of life. After five years of walking, stumbling, learning down this path of spiritual formation, I find that my relationship to grief, dying, death, and funerals has changed. My interaction with these mortal processes focuses less on external ministry skills and more on actions that grow from a deeply rooted devotional setting. In the second half of life—out of the second self—all things are worship supported by the practices of spiritual seeking.

Absorbing Pain and Leaving Hope: Carrying the Death and Resurrection of Jesus into Places of Grief

Christians are meant to carry the presence of Jesus into every situation. Having a sense of the grace in the ministry of Jesus enables us to be servants in times of crisis. We have the ability to imagine Christ walking with us, or walking as us, into difficult situations of all kinds. The language of 2 Corinthians chapters 4 and 5 describes this ministry:

"We always carry around in our body the death of Jesus, so that the life of Jesus may also be revealed in our body" (2 Cor. 4:10).

This is parallel to "I have been crucified with Christ and I no longer live, but Christ lives in me. The life I now live in the body, I live by faith in the Son of God, who loved me and gave himself for me" (Gal. 2:20).

As God's people, we are in Christ and Christ is in us. Our ministry in crisis is the ministry of Christ within us. Paul says of his ministry with the Corinthians that he is a simple clay pot filled with the power of God for the sake of others. He bore the presence of Jesus into the lives of others.

Therefore, we are free to enter any life situation with Christ in us as our guide and comfort. We can imagine that our own body—our own life, with its fears and preferences—can be laid aside as we let Jesus in us hear the awful news, view the dead body, sit with the wailing child. We are not desensitized; rather, we are in the moment with the very best of ourselves and the very best of God.

Christ's incarnational ministry continues when he becomes flesh again in us. The love of Jesus calls us out of our comfort zones into ministry. "For Christ's love compels us, because we are convinced that one died for all, and therefore all died. And he died for all, that those who live should no longer live for themselves but for him who died for them and was raised again" (2 Cor. 5:14–15).

Ministry is not just serving others. Christian ministry is serving others out of the example and energy of the death and resurrection of Jesus. His love compels us to serve others in terrible situations with great love in our hearts because Jesus came into our world with just such a heart, embracing us and the cross with great love. We are free to minister in life's danger zones because we are assured that the One who invites us into self-emptying ministry waits with the promised resurrection victory.

So when someone asks how we do what we do in ministry to the dying and the grieving, we answer that the love of Christ compels us, the dying of Christ teaches us, the resurrection of Christ comforts us. We do not do anything ourselves. It is Christ at work in us.

God has blessed me through the crucible of my fears. Now when I go into a crisis environment, especially in which life and death are at stake, I feel myself relax and slow down. All this is the gift of God. I have learned to see this gift in the context of God's broader work in my life.

All of us in Christ are on a journey with Jesus and in community with others in Christ. We cannot know as the journey begins where it will take us. We just know that we must sojourn with the risen Lord. In many ways, we are like Saul when Christ called him. Ananias was shocked that Jesus would think he could call Saul at all, much less call him to be his chosen instrument to take the good news to the Gentiles. The last sentence of the Lord's response to Ananias should reverberate in our hearts: "I will show him how much he must suffer for my name" (Acts 9:16). Truly, along the journey, we learn to bear the pain of ministry for the sake of Christ—without whining.

Notes

[1]Richard Rohr, *Falling Upward: A Spirituality for the Two Halves of Life* (San Francisco: Jossey-Bass, 2011).

[2]Ruth Haley Barton, *Sacred Rhythms* (Downers Grove, IL: InterVarsity Press, 2006).

[3]Ernest Becker, *The Denial of Death* (New York: Free Press, 1973).

Ministry to the One Dying

Life is real. People are mortal. Mortals die.

Since the work of this book began, I have been beside a family in our church dealing with stage four pancreatic cancer. The husband received the diagnosis. The diagnosis sent aftershocks through his wife, his sons, his sister, and his brother-in-law. Really, the whole church was traumatized. I found myself with the husband and wife as the facts of the cancer became known. I sat in conversations about chemotherapy. The husband wanted to visit with me about his decision to discontinue further treatment. The wife, our dear church bookkeeper and ministry assistant, needed to visit about the sudden plundering of her husband's life. She needed my ears for her words, my heart for her grief, and, occasionally, my shoulders to absorb her tears. The day came when John died. Becki and her sons and their wives were left with the memories of a good Christian man. We all met over a week to share stories, tears, laughter, and hugs to prepare the funeral. Even as I write this, the journey continues as Becki has returned for a few days of work. As ministers of comfort in the shadow of death, we commit to caravan with the dying and their loved ones to do the thing that love demands—be present.

The function of the church is not to create within itself an alternate reality empty of pain, separation, loss, or death. The fellowship of the church should be the most real, most authentic people and spiritual location on earth. In the church, people should be free to live well and to die well, without walls of denial or illusions of endless health. When the minister helps the church become this kind of body, he or she has done great work in ministering to a mortal community.

One of the key assumptions about ministry to the dying is that it includes everyone in the congregation every day. Understanding this reality helps the minister remember that every person in every pew is mortal. The mortal brokenness of life shows itself everywhere. Bodies wear down. Faces wrinkle. Diseases come. Injuries weaken. Depression and anxiety stalk the pews. Many of us minister in five-generation churches where the phases and finality of mortality are clear.

Everyone in church deals with the fear of death at some level. Some of our most destructive habits, attitudes, angers, and actions grow out of our attempts to deny death and cover over the fear of our own mortality. The minister must remember to keep our human mortality before the church by preaching the cross, studying difficult biblical texts, lamenting in worship, and praying openly for one another in physical trials. This kind of ministry helps prevent the church from becoming a servant of success, health, wealth, and politics. The church of Jesus should take on its shoulders his cross-bearing way of ministry. No one bearing a cross forgets his or her own mortality or the mortal loads of others.

Being Present When Presence Is the Most Important Thing

News that a member of the church is sick, perhaps terminally ill, often rocks the entire body, but the news most specifically affects the one whose life is threatened and that person's immediate family. The minister's general ministry to the congregation of the mortal quickly shifts its focus to a person for whom the distant someday of mortality has become a looming someday soon. Often, the minister hears the early hints of bad news before the church does. So many times, a dear one has shared with me that she has a suspicious shadow on a mammogram or that his blood just isn't right or that suddenly she has a limp out of the blue or vision that is blurred. We live in a world where the test result comes in, the heart cath is read, and the shadow on the mammogram or MRI becomes the shadow of the valley of death.

Being present through the early phases of breaking bad news is significant ministry. All of these moments of presence help the minister to serve well the one who is sick or injured. The next chapter will discuss ministry to the family in more depth. For now, we focus on the minister's ability to establish a relationship with the patient that will begin with the earliest indications of trouble and extend to the patient's last moment in this world. Being the minister in these times means being present with people in these times. The minister does not get this kind of bad news and just file it away. Dire news for others puts ministers to work. The minister cannot say, "I'll be praying for you," and not actually show up. The most important words in ministry are these: BE PRESENT.

Be present to be with. Be present to listen. Be present with families in waiting rooms while tests are going on. Be present to be quiet. Be present to pray, with words if necessary. At our house, we have a saying: Always go.

In whatever way the person and family will allow it, be present when tests of major body systems are being done. Be ready to be in the room when members of the medical staff discuss possible courses of action. The minister is not being pushy when he asks a person if she would like for him to go to the doctor with her. Recently, I got a CAT scan on my heart. My family doctor referred me to a cardiologist. My wife had to be out of town. I asked a dear and trusted friend from church to go with me to the appointment to be another set of ears for me. I had been that person for so many others that I knew how important it was to depend on someone— ministers must remember they, too, are people who need support.

Being present and being able to be quiet while present are ministry skills that elude many. Some ministers aren't comfortable enough with their own mortality to be able to stand in a mortal moment without generating diversions or making the moment about themselves. A minister does not have to be the loudest, most clever, most overtly holy person in the room all the time. Being the quiet presence of Jesus, representing his people in a time of family crisis, is more than enough. Perhaps you have been in a surgical waiting room and heard a minister rattle on for hours, telling inane stories to fill the time. It is fine to tell a few stories. However, a good test of one's personal waiting-room behavior requires asking oneself now and then, "Whose voices have been heard most in the past half hour or hour?" If the answer is the minister's voice, then the minister should take a turn at being quiet. It is better to be quieter and ask family members gentle questions and let them do the talking, letting them share their feelings and fears.

For a minister to be quiet in a room, she must have a quiet place in her heart. She must have made some peace with her own mortality. The minister must have moved past the inner compulsion to explain the present work or suspicious absence of God in the life of the patient. The minister must believe that God was present in the situation before she got there and will remain with the one suffering even after she leaves.

The commitment to minister to the dying and their families often stretches over an extended length of time. The minister to the dying one must have an attentive ear to the present and an eye on the horizon. This walk with the dying can bring pastors trying days and long journeys. Galatians 6:9 should be tattooed somewhere near our hearts: "Let us not become weary in doing good, for at the proper time we will reap a harvest if we do not give up."

Several years ago, a dear woman working in our office developed headaches and some instability. The scans showed a growth in her brain. I waited with the family on the second floor of St. David's Medical Center during the biopsy procedure. The doctor called the family together, and we heard the diagnosis: glioblastoma multiforme. The family wondered what that diagnosis meant. I didn't wonder; I knew it was the most dangerous of the brain tumors. Immediately, I knew no medical cure existed. The doctors could suggest radiation and chemotherapy, but without a direct intervention of God, no cure would come. Our dear one was dying. With that somber announcement in the hospital hallway, a journey with the family began that ended with our holding hands around Janet's bed, praying a prayer of blessing and release so she could let go of our hands and grasp the Father's. Ministers must have the ability to sustain loving care for others over a long time.

The effective minister will be available for conversations with the dying one when the possibility that something is really wrong is just a shadow. In these times, the minister may know more than the sick person knows. Ministers very often have been with many sick people, understand the medical language, and are experienced with the usual trajectory of many diseases. That presence will continue through the diagnostic process. The minister may be honored and burdened with an invitation to be present when the doctor shares the hard news with the patient. Especially as the prospect of bad news increases, the minister should offer to accompany the sick person to the doctor's visit.

Several things make the minister's presence important when hard news is delivered.

The minister will always share an "I was there with you when you heard the news" bond with the sick person. The minister will be present to minister immediately to the sick person or the family when the news is delivered. I never know how a person will react. I never know how family members will react. Some are stoic. Some fall apart. All reactions are legitimate and not to be judged.

The minister will listen well to the doctor's words and be able to repeat them to the sick person and the family when the doctor has gone. In countless situations, I have been asked, "What did she say?" when the doctor left the room. This is a time to repeat what the doctor said in an unembellished way. Often, the doctor will use medical terms that the family and the sick person do not understand. If the minister knows what those terms mean, translating medical or technical terms into more understandable words is genuinely helpful, though care should be taken not to make assumptions about one's level of understanding. When my wife was diagnosed with breast cancer, we learned acronyms and medical terms that we had never known before. In the years since, I have heard myself explain those terms to others who were as clueless and confused as we were in those first moments of staring death in the face. If the minister can help people know what the doctor said, that is good ministry.

The Journey of Dying

The journey of dying begins with the first, subtle indication that something is wrong. God has designed our psyches to deal with hard news in ways that slow down the impact of the news and blunt it, at least for a while. In *On Death and Dying,* Elisabeth Kübler-Ross proposed the well-known stages of grief experienced by a person facing a terminal diagnosis: denial, anger, bargaining, depression, and finally acceptance.[1] After her book was published and until her own death, others argued with her and even proposed more stages in the grief process. Without getting into the academic rough-and-tumble, let me say that the process includes at least the five stages that Kübler-Ross laid out. To minister effectively, the minister must know how these stages function in the life of the dying.

Facing death is hard. The first response to a terminal diagnosis is usually denial. One cannot receive such news and just say, "Fine," then go on with life. Often, denial is apparent as the dying one doubts the test results, wonders if a second or third opinion might clear up this mistaken diagnosis, wonders if some fly-by-night medical center in a third world country might have a cure. "This can't be happening to me" is a simple statement of denial. A minister can only respond to such statements of denial with comments like:

"I know. I can't believe it either."

"If you want to talk to another doctor, what could it hurt?"

Or sometimes it is right to say, "That news is so hard to hear," and then be quiet.

The compassionate minister never says, "You shouldn't feel that way" or "Are you kidding? It is time to set your house in order!" The fact that people get to have a bit of time in denial blesses them. Properly seen, a season of denial is a grace, not a curse. Reality waits. There is time enough for reality.

A dying person may vent anger about the unfairness of the diagnosis. Plans for the future are now out of reach. The anticipated future of being present for a spouse, children, or grandchildren has evaporated. The God who provides seems to have empty pockets; he seems unmoved by prayers offered in faith and in abundance. Anger may emerge as heated regret for actions that cannot be undone, relationships that cannot be repaired, a walk with Christ that began so late. Anger expressed by a dying person can be hard to hear, but the minister must remember that the anger ultimately is a fulminating question for God and God alone.

Usually, the anger toward others doesn't last long, but sometimes a dying person can say hurtful things to family members or others. The minister understands that it's not helpful to lecture the dying person, but he may have to have a conversation with those who were wounded. They know the person is dying, but their words sting nonetheless. Help them reframe the comments: "She's learning to face her own death." "We give grace here." "Don't leave. It won't last."

Often, the dying one is angry with God. In 1976, my Albuquerque Police Department chaplaincy training officer, Jack Price, told me: "Don't ever try to talk anyone out of being angry at God. People have been angry at God for centuries. He can handle it." Those words hold up today. Stay present for the angry dying one. The anger will pass. Do not try to explain what God is doing. You don't know.

Bargaining for a better deal is a natural stage of grief for the dying. In bargaining, one seeks to barter with God for healing or more time: "I'll start reading my Bible every day if you will make me well." "I'll give everything I have to the church if you will make me well." "Just let me live until my daughter graduates from high school, and then I'll go quietly." Hezekiah's request for an extension to his life illustrates a bargaining heart (2 Kings 20). A sensitive minister meets and accepts a person's feelings where he or she is. To someone proposing some kind of repentance as a bargain, I have said gently, and with a smile, that maybe that change of heart or life or behavior might be a good idea anyway. To those proposing that God give them time to experience some benchmark in life, like the future marriage of a daughter, the birth of a grandchild, or one more trip to some sentimental spot, I have replied, "Wouldn't that be sweet. I hope you get to do that." Be gentle with the dying who seek to bargain with God.

Inevitably, depression comes. Finally, when the denial won't hold, the anger is unsustainable, and no bargain has been achieved, the abyss appears—black, cold, unrelenting: "My God, my God, why have you forsaken me?" The prepared, courageous minister sits in the presence of a depressed saint with great love in his or her heart, but few words. These are moments for meaningful touch. Holding someone's hand can bring comfort. Letting someone cry hot tears into your shoulder is an act of Christian mercy. In these moments, I have tried to avoid giving glib assurances. I don't beat up a depressed dying one with our hope in Christ. Sometimes I don't offer to pray with the one in such darkness. It can be unseemly to flaunt one's hope in the presence of a depressed, dying person. Any statement beginning with "Now you know . . ." that intends to lecture a dying person because he is underperforming some standard of external religiosity needs to stop in my throat before I speak. I believe only God has the right to enter some dark places. The dying have the right to mourn their own deaths. Be present. Pray the prayers of your heart. This kind of depression does not need to be fixed; it needs to be weathered, lived through, accompanied.

Kübler-Ross describes acceptance as a final giving in to the fact of one's death and a sense that one's dying is in the natural order of things. Kübler-Ross included in her book quotes from Bengali poet and artist Rabindranath Tagore that indicated a certain self-satisfaction with letting one's bit of soul rejoin the great soul of the universe. This pantheistic version of hope from the

East is a far cry from the fullness of Christian hope that heralds victory over death and the survival of the individual into the presence of God. Emerging from the underbrush of facing one's own death and coming into the light of hope in the risen Jesus is more than acceptance of death. It is the acceptance of victory over death through Christ.

One of my role models in life was Robert (Bob) Vance. He preached Jesus in Germany after World War II. He and I traveled to Argentina and Russia together, encouraging missionaries and young churches. He was one of my elders in Abilene, Texas. Bob was diagnosed with an aggressive cancer. He wrestled with it in various ways, working through the Kübler-Ross stages in his own way. Finally, one day during a visit, he told me that he was not going to pursue any further curative treatment. He said with clear eyes and a firm voice, "You know, Eddie, eventually we have to live like we believe all this."

Yes, we do; and coming to that point is Christian acceptance.

When Death Comes Suddenly

The path of dying described by Kübler-Ross is more or less typical for those of all ages who receive a bad diagnosis. Children seem to come to acceptance and hope sooner than adults do. However, not all dying leaves time for angry words and thoughtful reflection.

When Death Is Sudden and Close

One of my best friends, a prominent physician, an elder in our church with whom I talked every day for twenty years, suddenly died of a heart attack while on vacation with his family. He was my friend, but I was also his minister and his family's minister, and it was my responsibility to minister to his family, friends, and the church where we had served together. He was only fifty-five. I have ministered in the aftermath of death and performed funerals for my in-laws and my parents, but this was harder. Yet, if you have a certain set of gifts and graces, you absorb the dimensions of the moment. You learn to say, "I know what this is. I know this is beyond me."

Some things must be done in such circumstances in spite of yourself and your own grief because the Lord has given you experiences that will help you immerse yourself in the moment. Then sometimes, ministry is knowing what not to do. When David died, there came the moment when his body was ready to be seen. At least two dozen people filled the room. Everyone was crying. The sorrow was so present, so overwhelming, that I chose to free the grief and not suppress it by interrupting with wise words or even a prayer. God could hear the cries of the people in that room. He did not need my intervention.

Later, I went when no one else was there and stood in the room with David. I took that personal time to mourn. I couldn't bleed all the emotion out of me because I had work to do—ministry to do—but I had to spend some personal time with my friend as well in order to serve his family. I cried and cried.

Sudden death is all too common. On countless days, I would get the phone call to come to some brother's or sister's home where death had come suddenly. Walking into the house, nursing home, or hospital room where a sudden death has occurred is a time for centering prayer and spiritual courage. You look at death in the face of one you know and love. Your own grief wells up. You have no way of knowing what the outpouring of sudden grief will look like. You must be ready for anything.

The deceased has not experienced the stages of loss in the time frame of moments or even a few days, but that grief work will be dumped onto the family and friends in a sudden, unrelenting way.

When called to the scene of a suicide, the minister enters the scene of the worst sudden death. Suicide is a desperate act meant to end pain, express anger, or somehow remove the burden of one's life from the concern of others. The thought process of the suicidal person is very inward. It probably seems rational to the one making the decision, but irrational to those who love and care about the one in personal darkness.

Suicide was once considered an unforgivable sin, since one murdered himself, leaving no opportunity for absolution. This Roman Catholic position was tacitly held by many. Once, when called to the home of a Catholic family whose twenty-two-year-old son had taken his life, the family asked me to call their priest to see if their son could have a funeral mass in the church. In the conversation with a wise and kind priest, he told me that he knew the older Catholic position on suicide, but now suicide is considered an irrational act of an unbalanced person. That person would not be held accountable for that final, irrational act. The family was invited to have the funeral mass.

This is where our hearts should be in the suicide setting. We must have compassion for the one who is dead and even more of a loving embrace for the family and friends left empty-armed.

Regardless of the cause of the sudden death, as the minister, you are expected to know what to do when sudden death comes. Some authority—doctor, nurse, coroner—will have to come and certify the death. When moving to a new town, learn what the legal requirements are. A local funeral director or physician will be able to help you learn the local requirements and routine.

In the case of a suicide, law enforcement will be involved as well, and an autopsy may be required. Know what the law requires in the state where you live. If the funeral home must come for the body, that may be a difficult decision if the deceased and family had never talked about such decisions. A family may ask the minister which funeral home to call. A minister doesn't need to be in a community very long before he knows which funeral homes treat the dead and the family with compassion and respect. Have two good choices to suggest, and stay with the family at least until the body has been removed.

Books have been written on these stages and others. Read some of them and remember, even though the stages of grief are listed in some order, that does not mean they will be experienced in that order or even one at a time. It does mean that the Christian minister will need to pray for the wisdom and insight to meet the dying on their ground and to stand inside the inner circle of their lives as they process the loss of their lives.

Present in Holy Moments

The Chinese philosopher Lao Tzu said a journey of a thousand miles begins with a single step. A journey of a thousand miles also ends with a single step. Ministers to the dying are willing to be present with the ones they have pastored to this final hour and with their families when the last moment comes.

With increasing frequency, these moments come in a hospice setting. Hospice care blesses the dying and their families by providing palliative care in a deeply compassionate way. Hospice nurses and attendants and any hospice-related chaplains are always very, very helpful. Their constant focus is on the quality of life available to the dying. Getting well is no longer a priority; the priority is getting through the task of dying with dignity and comfort. The minister finds fellow ministers in the hospice staff. Always give them the respect and encouragement they need and deserve as they do their work. Minister to the dying one, to the family, and to the hospice staff.

After experiencing those last hours a few times with the dying and their families, ministers learn the characteristic Cheyne-Stokes pattern of interrupted breathing that often precedes death by twenty-four to thirty-six hours. The subtle changes in pulse and respiration rates on a vital signs monitor or the visible pulse points on the scalp or neck give an indication of where the person is in the process. These are holy moments among Christians.

Often, in these last moments, families gather around the dying loved one and pray the prayer of release. The prayer of release allows the family to pray blessing and thanksgiving, thanking God for the life of the one whose life is ending and blessing the departing into the presence of God. The sweetest of these prayers include words to the loved one saying, "We have loved you. You have loved us. You have given us what we have needed. We have our lives. We have your love. You have done everything you needed to do. There is nothing else in this world that you need to do. Before God and in his love, we release you into the love and comfort of the Father. Go. All is well."

And then death comes. Two moments in life are most awe-inspiring: the time between the birth and the first breath of a baby and the first moments after the last breath of a sainted man or woman. I cannot remember all the last breaths I have witnessed. I recently attended my mother and then my father as they died. We watched and we waited for the deep silence of the moment of death. It came.

Ministers help people journey from first to last breath. When that last breath expires and the folks from the funeral home take the body out of the room, the ministry to that dying one is accomplished. Many lessons have been learned. Although the minister's heart is torn with the pain of death and loss, it overflows with thanks to God for his companionship in this ministry to the dying.

Note

[1]Elisabeth Kübler-Ross, *On Death and Dying* (New York: Scribner, 1969).

Ministry to the Family
of the One Dying

People are unique. No one death is like any other. Family and friends of the deceased are also unique. People are at their best and worst in times of stress. The minister will never be able to anticipate exactly what a family will need. No book could contain all the possible variations of ministry needed by families.

In the last chapter, we identified the one dying as the most important person in the focus of the minister's service. As true as that is, the minister will spend as much or more time with the family of the dying one—and those interactions are almost always more complicated than the relationship with the one dying. In this chapter, we will block out some aspects of essential ministry to families to help them through the journey of grief and consider some especially challenging people who may be a part of the family. Sometimes this is ministry in a minefield.

When the first indications arise that a life-threatening condition is at work, the news is shared first with those closest to the threatened one and soon with the rest of the family. The minister must be ready to react with love and care to each person in the family. These settings are seldom easy, and the many situations that present themselves are among the reasons ministers pray for wisdom.

When the bad news hits, the minister begins—or perhaps expands and deepens—a relationship with the family of the sick one, making note of all the members of the family who are present and those who are not. Parents, spouses, ex-spouses, children, siblings, aunts and uncles, nephews and nieces, and friends who function as family can all have remarkably close attachments to the patient. They can also be stunningly, inexplicably distant. The minister must have a good list of the actors in this real-life drama. I once walked through a dying, then grieving process with a family, got to the funeral, and found out about a brother who had never been mentioned. He was there for the service, but he was not happy about his older brother having completely left him out of the funeral planning—not a good moment. I made a note to always ask the funeral director for a complete list of the surviving family before going very far in planning a funeral.

Even when the minister has a long relationship with a family, she cannot always anticipate where the strengths and weaknesses in a family lie; but rest assured that the stress of facing the imminent death of one of their own inevitably reveals the fault lines in the family structure. The minister must serve over and around those fault lines in caring for the family and their sick one. The minister must pay attention to ways she might avoid being triangulated into conflicted relationships by adopting a calm presence, being engaged but not enmeshed with the family, and certainly not becoming an ally of any particular faction of the family that may be setting itself against some other family group.

When the minister walks into the room where loved ones of the dying person have gathered, he must get the feel of the room—and of where each person in the room seems to be. Who's in charge? Who's engaged? Who's withdrawn? Knowing what to do and what to say depends entirely on what you find there. The minister cannot enter the room with an agenda or a certain set of things he plans to do, but should instead go with a set of tools he may use in response to what he finds. If you walk in and everyone's quiet—then you're quiet for a while too. Join those gathered wherever they are. In some way, do a check-in with each person. This doesn't have to be intensive, but get a verbal response from each person in order to get an indication of where they are. Make it a point to maintain meaningful contact with the least communicative person or people in the room. This will require you to work against your natural affinity that will probably be to converse with those who are more comfortable in the conversation and allow them to set all the priorities for your ministry. Resist that more comfortable place and reach out to the quieter, angrier, more hurting people.

An amazing aspect of ministry to a family of one dying is how the stages of grief suddenly begin to operate in the family members. All of the stages—anger, denial, bargaining, depression, acceptance, and hope—will begin as the bad news hits. Each family member will be different, with her or his own starting place in dealing with the awful news. The minister walks into a room with a patient in denial, a wife in anger, a child who is bargaining, and a mother in depression all at the same time.

No matter how many families a minister has served, he must pray each time he begins again for wisdom to identify very early in conversations where people are in their grief. The sooner one knows what stage a person is in, the sooner he can begin responding appropriately. Even if two or more people are in the same stage of grief, no two will express it in the same way. People in different stages of grief can really annoy one another and pass judgment on another's love for the sick family member. I can't count how many times I have been asked by family members who are in anger to go talk some sense into the sick one or another family member who is stuck in denial. That doesn't work. No one can police the grief response of any other person—not even the minister.

In working with families in these situations, the responsibility of the minister is to accept and to communicate acceptance to every person, wherever they are in their grief work. The first great tool of acceptance is listening. An open question as simple as "So how are you today?" gives the family member permission to talk and creates space for the minister to listen actively, standing within the circle of that person's stage of grief. You must do this even if it requires you to suspend what you are sure you know. I have been in conversations with folks whose loved one had advanced pancreatic cancer and heard them go deep in denial as they talked of exotic treatments in faraway locations. In my own heart, I was saying, "No. That is not going to be helpful. You are going to waste the few good days your loved one has left chasing some therapy that will do little, if any, good. And even if it prolongs life, it will only prolong the length and depth of the suffering."

I was saying that to myself because those were not remarks for me to share. My responsibility was to nod and ask questions about the course of action so the conversation would continue. My responsibility was to feel their ache in my heart and to pray with them on the ground on which they stood. Jesus wept with Mary and Martha on the way to the tomb of Lazarus, even though he knew Lazarus would be walking back to the house with them. We cannot let any truth we know or that we think we know keep us from the weeping—from our most appropriate response to those in their grief.

Someone inevitably will ask, "Who is going to tell them the truth and tell them to face it!" Don't worry about the truth. The truth will come. These stages of grief are just the gifts God gave us to enable us to absorb brutally bad news over a period of time. Ministering to people in their various stages of grief actually gives them the support and blessing needed to move a bit closer to acceptance and hope. Trying to argue people out of the stage they are in or, worse, accusing them of being thoughtless, shallow, or unfaithful by thinking the way they are, is the surest way to cause a person to get stuck in a stage longer and more destructively than they should.

The minister does not rescue people from their grief. The minister shepherds them through it.

Miscarriage: A Real Life and a Real Death

Heartache. Heartbreak.

The church does not know how to minister to the grief that grows from miscarriage. We have no rituals to announce these losses. We have no rituals to gather around the grief, weep with the emptiness, hug the pain. In many ways, this vacancy of ministry is traceable to the fact of male leadership and male clergy in many of our churches. Churches have had little if any formal way of ministering to women in their deepest pain. We need to do better.

Miscarriage is a real loss of a real life. When a couple finds out they are expecting a child, they immediately begin living into the reality of life with the child growing between them. They imagine the journey of the pregnancy, the joy of their parents, the changes in the wife's body, the way the house will need to be altered, the birth, the first step, the first day of school, Little League, Girl Scout cookies. . . . And then the baby's life ends. All the dreams die.

The women who have talked to me protest the language used to describe the end of their babies' lives. "Miscarriage" and "lost your baby" make it sound like they were inattentive in some way. They were not careless with their babies. The things that people say are so inane and hurtful: "God decided it wasn't your time." "God needed another angel in heaven."

Well-meaning people say terrible things when they should be quiet and just hug someone aching from loss.

The challenge, one I have not met as I write, is to work with the church, and especially the women who have experienced the loss of an unborn child, to create acknowledgment-of-loss rituals and ceremonies of life, loss, and grief to wrap around those who have lost a baby in such a way.

This is very important when the loss of the life is late enough in the pregnancy to require an actual burial. I have met young couples in cemeteries where in nearly solitary grief we have prayed over tiny caskets of broken dreams, buried them deep, and aimlessly wandered back to life. People need more love than that. The church needs to be more attentive than that. As ministers, we need to step up.

Always Go

When death is imminent, the family comes together. Often, the minister will be invited or expected to be present. Always go. If you have been walking along with the family, they will want you there at the end. Even if the family has asked that this be a "family only" time, they will usually want the minister who has been faithful to them there. If it is at all possible, be present when death comes. Ministry to the family in the hospital room, hospice, or home is very much the same ministry: sharing meaningful conversation, sitting quietly, singing hymns, offering prayer, gathering the family for and leading a prayer of release.

Except for very rare occasions or with very small families, the whole family will rarely be present when their loved one dies. One of the blessings that comes with the minister present at the death is that the minister can tell the story of how the death occurred to those who were not there. This is especially important when some aspect of those moments is comforting or unexpectedly sweet. Telling those who were not there about how death came can be an important act of ministry: grandmother held on until all her children could be around her bed; the dear aunt seemed to be shy about dying in front of family, so she waited until those gathered had all walked out into the hallway and then slipped away. Only eyewitnesses can tell these stories well. Ministers should be eyewitnesses to such moments of loss and grace.

After death comes, stay with the family until the body is removed. Waves of grief will likely roll through the family shortly after the death. You may need to shepherd the family through those intense aftershock moments.

AND: Allow Natural Death

DNR is among the ominous terms that narrate the care of the sick and the dying. For many, posting the DNR to a loved one's care protocol is very difficult. By its "Do Not," it appears that legitimate things that could be done for the patient just aren't going to be done. How does a loving person deny another person access to resuscitation? No doubt, this involves making a serious judgment about the quality of life available to the patient if resuscitation sustained life.

The bind created by the language calling for a denial of care led the late Rev. Chuck Meyer, a chaplain and vice president of St. David's Medical Center in Austin, Texas, to call for different language in cases of diminishing quality of life with no hope of reversal. Meyer advocated using AND—Allow Natural Death—as the position of the family and medical staff with regard to the patient. A time comes when no healing can bring back meaningful life. A time comes when dying *is* the only healing from the pain and disorientation. A time comes to Allow Natural Death. The human body knows how to die if no one gets in the way. The minister must admit that such a time can come in every life. The minister may be asked by the family, "What do you think about setting a DNR on Momma?" Then is a good time to mention gently that AND may be a better way of thinking about the DNR request, even if the facility or medical professionals in charge are not using that terminology.

Every Family Has at Least One

While this general overview of the ministry to a family of one dying should serve as a helpful introduction to the tasks of ministry, a few special people need to be mentioned, because they can be especially disruptive and might require the minister's well-timed words.

The relative-on-the-Internet can be difficult. For many years, people relied on the medical expertise of the doctors in their immediate area. With better transportation and communication, people were able to seek second opinions and, possibly, better care elsewhere. Now the Internet allows people to send themselves to Google Medical School. The member of the family who sets up the computer in the room and uses it to question and second-guess every move made by the doctors and nurses is practicing a form of denial.

I have experienced family members questioning all medications by raising all of the possible reactions to the drugs and then noting random, rare reactions rumored to have occurred: there was that man in Fiji who grew a horn while receiving that medicine. This Google practitioner questions decisions and actions of the doctors, the work of the nurses, the quality of the hospital, and on and on and on. All this is an attempt to be the hero who rescues the sick, beloved one.

This urge to help find the best care for the sick one doesn't come from an evil place in a person's heart, but this behavior isn't helpful. The minister must be gentle. I have responded in these situations by gently questioning what outcome the Google practitioner is expecting. Does he really think the doctors on the case are out of touch with current treatment protocols? I have also made it a point to have separate conversations with the doctors to assure them that the family supports their work and that I am ready to intervene more forcefully if the doctor asks. Most doctors know how to establish their own boundaries, but every doctor or nurse I have had this conversation with really appreciated knowing the minister was not a fan of the troublesome behavior.

Because of the mobile age we live in, most families have a close relative from out of town. Often, this relative shows up and suddenly wants to question the care being given and take the reins from those who have been faithfully caring for their sick family member, sometimes for years. My good friend Dr. David Bailey introduced me to this bullying behavior. He said that you could tell there was going to be trouble when the out-of-town relative hit the hospital. David said that he got to where he would take them aside privately and say, "Okay, I know you are feeling guilty because of all you have done to avoid giving your [mom, dad, brother, sister, pick one] the love and attention that you should have. I know you feel guilty for pushing all the care off on your [pick a family member]. So here is the deal: Your other family members have this under good control. All that can be done is being done. Now you can settle down and be quiet and be helpful, or you can go home. You decide, but you cannot do this!"

I believe that a variation of this little speech should be in every minister's repertoire. It is not uncommon for someone in a family to have avoided treating their loved one right and foisted that care responsibility off on others. Certainly, not every relative who lives in a distant location follows this pattern, but the minister will quickly recognize those who do and can help everyone, including the invading sibling, cousin, or child, by intervening.

The "don't be sad because everything is all right because we are Christians" person is living in denial too. This form of denial is hard on people, because this person implies by his very presence that his faith is great and the faith of the grieving others is flawed and inadequate. These folks are quick to talk about the rightness of what God is doing in the life of the one suffering. They are too glib about God needing the dying person in heaven and too quick to equate expressions of grief with a lack of faith. The minister needs to visit with this person to persuade him to throttle back the confident God talk. Even things that are true can be harsh and unloving when said at the wrong time and in the wrong way. This person needs to learn to express faith in God through loving, quiet companionship with the brokenhearted. The brokenhearted need shoulders, not sermons.

The cast of characters gathered around one dying often includes "the one who did him wrong." Often, the actions of a grown son or daughter created distance in the relationship with a dying parent. The minister may actually hear the story or just sense the tension in the relationship. Since our work is a ministry of reconciliation, the minister seeks to create a moment for healing between two people before one of them dies. This process starts with the minister offering an I-message to the offending one: "I notice that there is something that I can't quite put my finger on going on between you and your father. Would you mind telling me about it?"

If the offending person will let the minister in and tell the story, then the minister is in a position to help bring healing. This is such a precious ministry. I was about to help with a funeral service in a little town east of Abilene. I walked down the hall toward the viewing room where the man's casket was. I heard a voice as I approached the doorway. "Why did you die! Why did you die! I never got the chance to tell you I was sorry." As I looked into the room, the man's youngest daughter, who was in her midtwenties, was broken with grief and unresolved guilt. What a gift a moment of reconciliation between the two of them would have been.

Amid this cast of characters, in almost every context, you'll find at least one person you would call "the rock." It could be the one who has worked through his or her own grief or who has the capacity to delay it in order to serve the needs of the situation. Usually, it will be an individual of personal faith who has experience with the one who has died—who knew and accepted that person as they really were with few illusions and no hidden anger. As a result, they can be as clear-headed and available to help as anyone can be.

That person is the one the minister should go to and offer a private moment to say, "I see you and what you're doing, and it's so valuable." It's important to say, "I see you."

Often, this will be the nearest person unrelated by blood to the deceased. And often it may be one of the children. Though usually not all the children are helpful, often one will be. This is a place where the family that has a faith community typically has more stable people around than one that doesn't.

Ministry in Christ calls for many gifts and graces. No minister has all the gifts and graces required to meet all the challenges that can arise in families in times of grief and loss. Still, we all should ask God for more and more wisdom and discernment as we enter these trying situations. To be sure, often the situations themselves are the schools that teach the graces and nurture the gifts.

Grief Isn't Always about Dying

Sometimes grief is present when death is not the problem. Life is.

Divorce. Bankruptcy. Losing a job. Encountering a change of health that will not be fatal but that will be life-changing. Losing a family home to fire or a natural disaster, or even losing a pet.

Devastating loss doesn't always lead to the cemetery. In fact, sometimes the path to acceptance is clearer after a death than on the twisted roads of life's other losses. The dark humor surrounding many conversations about divorce goes something like this: "The problem is that he didn't die. He keeps showing up."

While our work in these pages focuses on ministry to the dying and to the family of the dying, every minister will be called to serve and walk with those who are coming to terms with these other losses. The steps of grief will be very much the same. Anger, denial, or bargaining can take up long residence in the life of one whose plan for life has just been irrevocably changed. Well-meaning family members and loved ones may be just as helpful or unhelpful in their comments. The minister must understand and accept that for this person, the grief is as palpable as it is to the bereaved. Still the call is to go, to be present.

5

The Place of the Funeral in the Ministry of Comfort

As I am writing, a family is waiting for me to drop by their house to help plan the funeral for their husband and father who is under hospice care and in his last days with cancer. The funeral will be the last public statement from this family about the one they love so much. The planning for this last public word deserves the minister's best effort.

Traditions about the things that must be done at a funeral vary within different parts of the country, different faith communities, different ethnic communities, even different families. The template presented in this chapter is a reliable starting place for most funerals. More important than the form of the service, however, is the proper emphasis of the service, remembering that, unless otherwise indicated, this book deals with funerals inside the faith community.

Honoring Life as an Act of God

The life of the deceased is an act of God. God is at work in whatever a Christian becomes in his or her life. Good attitude and deeds proceed from the fruit of the Spirit. Honoring a person for being a good person because of excellent parents or a generally sunny disposition is fine. But somewhere we have to introduce the notion that no one is born this wonderful—her goodness is not just a credit to the people who bore and raised her. In the funeral, there must be the notion that this is a redeemed person. If she became something marvelous, it's because the Spirit in her life gave her gifts that she took into the community. She was not the source of her own greatness.

God works in many ways. But at the center of any good Christian life is a moment of dying to self and allowing God's resurrection power to begin a spiritual renewal that exceeds what any individual can achieve by human effort.

At the center of all Christian worship is the recitation of the acts of God. A funeral becomes worship as the deceased is honored as an act of God. The hope of life and resurrection must serve as the ending note of every funeral for a Christian. God has raised Jesus from the dead. The resurrection of Jesus was the first season of the great harvest of new life that will come at the end of all things (1 Cor. 15:22–23).

With the presence and power of God's work acknowledged, the secondary focus of the funeral is the life of the deceased. This may seem like an unnecessary thing to say, but too many times, a funeral is impersonal and cold. Recently, I attended a service for a woman. Some Christ-a-bap-litarian minister read a liturgy that had beautiful prayers and affirmations of faith, but he had no words about the woman who had died. The life of the faithfully deceased serves as the text of the funeral as surely as verses from the Bible are the text of a sermon.

The minister's task at the funeral is to exegete the person's life in some clear way that reveals how, in this man, woman, or child, Christ became flesh again. In preparing for the funeral, the minister will reflect on the challenges, defeats, and victories of the person's life. She will note when and where the person was born. Some birthdates and birthplaces mean that the person lived through trying times, through wars, through economic distress. Every generation has some identifying tendencies, some marker events.

A minister should know the ethos of the '50s, '60s, '70s, etc. She should know a little history. Knowing the culture and history of a community makes a difference and helps a minister to understand the stories of the people who make up that community. Did he live through or fight in Vietnam? Did she march in the civil rights protests of the '60s?

Have a sense of the person's place in his family of origin. He was the oldest son in a family of five siblings—what does that mean? She was the youngest daughter? Are there stories about that? Birth order can matter. The minister needs to be thoughtful about the broader context of a person's life and how that helped create the person that they were.

Reflecting on the structure of the family helps the minister know how to talk about an only child, the youngest of ten, or an orphan left alone in the world. The profession of the deceased will have shaped her or his life. The hobbies a person enjoyed reflect the priorities of life. Works of service in the family, church, and community are fingerprints the deceased has left behind. As the minister sits with the family, interviewing them, seeking stories, themes, and favorite Bible stories and verses that clarify the lived-out witness of their loved one, a hologram of memory begins to appear. Sometimes, getting to leaf through someone's personal Bible reveals favorite books and texts. A note written in the margin of a Bible may give the minister the theme for the funeral service. Discovering these facts and functions of a person's life unlocks the life text that the minister preaches.

With as much information as possible gathered, the minister should put on the shoes of the deceased and live his or her life in order to prepare the funeral remarks. This is why the minister must have worked through his or her own feelings about death. One who must live in denial of death to protect his or her own being will not have the freedom of spirit required to enter the life of the deceased and live that life down to its end. The minister lives and dies with every funeral.

Music plays a central role in most Christian funerals. The spoken parts of a funeral are usually framed or adorned with songs that confess the faith of the deceased and the hope of the family. I have had a few families tell me their mother or father didn't care much for singing and had no favorite songs. However, that is usually far from the case. For many of us, our songs express our faith far more eloquently than our words. Some of us would be happy to have our funerals be festivals of singing and singing only. The minister must ask the family what music it would like in the funeral and must try to include those songs if at all possible, whether sung by the congregation or offered by a group or soloist.

Secular songs may be very meaningful to a family. The minister does well to reserve judgment on the song choices and instead reflect on the facts of the family's life and love that make those songs seem so right. One of my good friends had Willie Nelson's "You Were Always on My Mind" played at the end of his funeral because it was a song he and his wife enjoyed so much. The song was appropriate to the moment. My friend and former elder Mark Tate sat on the front row of the church and played the banjo to honor his father Willard. In a funeral for a young mother who had done work in Great Britain, her husband wanted "Amazing Grace" on the bagpipes. At the end of the service, the bagpiper entered from a side door, walked to the front of the chapel, and played while walking slowly down the aisle and out of the building.

The minister owes the family the truth when someone suggests a really bad idea for music. Not everyone who volunteers to play or sing should. Awful music spoils the focus of the service on the deceased and the family. Good music can personalize, soothe, and inspire.

The minister does well who keeps the focus of the funeral on the work of God and specifically his work in his deceased servant. The minister will carefully balance the sorrow of loss, the thanksgiving for the life lived, and the joy in the hope of life eternal in the way most appropriate for the circumstances of the death and funeral.

At the end of the funeral, people should leave loving God more and being a bit more amazed at what God can do with people who put themselves in God's transforming hand.

A Plan for the Funeral

Usually, the minister plans the funeral service. Sometimes the family, or even the deceased, has preplanned the funeral and all the pieces are in place. That is almost always a blessing. When it's the minister's lot to plan the funeral, many variations in funeral services are possible, but the minister should have a standard funeral form that families can begin with in their planning. A good beginning outline for the speaking parts is:

- Welcome
- Prayer
- Reading of the obituary
- Eulogies
- Preaching the funeral sermon
- Benediction

The funeral should not be more than an hour. After an hour, people in the audience lose their focus. People have usually reserved an hour or so for the service. As the hour mark approaches and passes, they are no longer thinking about the deceased or the family but considering whether it would be rude to leave, if they dare be seen sending a text to the office to explain why they'll be late for that next meeting, or to someone who can pick up the kids from school. Instead of passing judgment on the scheduling and attention spans of those attending the funeral, the more loving and considerate goal is to plan the funeral inside of an hour. Even services for community leaders or elected officials or services for those lost in tragic ways are better if they are planned with discipline. Everything cannot be said during the funeral. Everyone cannot speak. All the comfort cannot be shared in one service. The funeral is a focused gathering of meaningful thoughts and experiences that frees people to love and care for the family after the funeral.

In the welcome, the minister expresses thanks from the family and the church for each person's attendance. The welcome can also be a good place to read Scripture that sets the tone for the rest of the service. If few people are available to help with the service, the minister will likely lead the opening prayer too. A funeral is bracketed by prayer, acknowledging God's benevolent presence at the beginning and the end—of the service and of our lives.

The reading of the obituary reminds everyone of the facts of the deceased's life. The obituary was usually produced to be published in the newspaper and online. Typically, the obituary is printed in a program that is handed out as guests arrive or sign the guest book. When it is merely read by someone, it always comes off a bit cold and detached, and unnecessary. In the context of the funeral, the obituary is always better if shared by someone who knew the deceased and who can add personal experiences to transform the sharing of the obituary from the reading of a document to the telling of a story. Sometimes this is not possible, but the funeral is much better when a life story is told.

Eulogies or words of tribute come after the obituary. The family will usually identify relatives and friends to share their memories of the deceased. These are best when the speakers represent different arenas of a person's life; three eulogies of five minutes each is ideal. If the service focuses on family, the tributes might be from a brother, a daughter, and a son-in-law or grandchild. If the tributes would be better from family, community or work, and church, then men or women from those different areas of life would speak. In working with the family to plan the funeral, the minister can ask questions that may help the family recall different aspects of the loved one's life. I recall the funeral of a woman who was deeply loved and admired by the colleagues whom she served with for more than thirty years, and who were the primary audience at the funeral. The family completely excluded this aspect of her life from the service, probably because of their exhaustion after caring for her through a painful decline and dementia.

When a family member plans to speak at the service, the minister should always be ready to step to the microphone and read for someone, or assist one who becomes too emotional to continue. Sometimes family members are unexpectedly and emotionally overcome and cannot present what they have written. The minister should always be ready to read for someone or even to step to the microphone and assist one who is overcome. This may be the place to add a warning against bad poetry written overnight by some friend or family member. People mean well, but if there is any way as a minister you can keep five minutes of "tears-fears, treats-feats, now-how" doggerel out of a funeral, you will have served the family well.

The funeral sermon or remarks are the minister's words for the family and the audience. This is not an evangelistic sermon, but it is good news. In many ways, the funeral sermon is a living thing that seeks to do several things:

- Tell the truth.
- Express the emotional dimensions of the moment.
- Speak of the nobility of a life lived in faith and service.
- Draw all into the hope offered to those who live by faith.

The experienced minister often hears something in one of the tributes that adds just a bit of insight into the deceased or the family that can be incorporated into his or her remarks, weaving together the themes that have been shared by the eulogists.

Telling the truth in the funeral sermon may call for a direct reference to the awfulness of death, to the difficulty of the long decline before death. It may call for a reflection on the loss of the loved one years ago as dementia burned down the memory, leaving only the physical shell of the life whose loss is now finally mourned. Whatever is the truest, non-hurtful thing that could be said to establish that this moment is not make believe or play-like must be said. I have often said at the beginning of funeral remarks, "We should not be here now!" and at other services, "Finally, finally, we are here." Both remarks were true in their context.

This commitment to saying what is true includes expressing the emotional dimensions of the moment and requires the minister to assess the right ratio of sorrow to joy. I can tell you that the funeral for a baby boy who died after a full-term birth has no room for joy in those minutes around that grave, and I can tell you that there is only a sliver of sorrow left for the great saintly man or woman who has lived into his or her nineties and has come to death full of faith and surrounded by his or her family. A godly person can live all the tragedy out of their death.

Emotionally Matching the Moment

Stand inside the deepest sorrow to speak halting lament and tear-stained hope, leaving no space for denial of death and sorrow. Do not choke back your tears. Weep out your words. But on the days of joyful celebration of a life lived long and well, when the family wants to celebrate life with stories and laughter, do not put on some somber ministerial funeral face. Doing so does not serve the family in that moment. I have found that in every funeral for a person of faith, laughter always has a place in the service. People feel free to tell stories that highlight the deceased person's balanced, delightful life. As the minister, you should feel free to let some laughter give the family and others a breath of fresh air in the midst of a difficult day. Of course, humorous stories and remarks must be disciplined so that they bring some aspect of the person's story to life. The minister senses the emotional temperature of the moment. A funeral is a mix of dirge and delight; lead it with great joy and spirit.

When speaking of the nobility of a life, the minister reminds a family and church that all life is precious and every life gives gifts to those around it. The life of a baby has already been the focal point of love. The death of a child is cruel, yet the child is a precious gift who will be a part of that family forever. The life of an adult Christian will have taken paths of service that have blessed family, friends, church, and community. The minister lifts up the life of the departed Christian as a sign of the continuing incarnation of Christ in the world.

Then finally the minister draws all into the resurrection hope offered to those who live by faith. This world is not our home; we are just passing through. We are free in Christ to anticipate reunion with those who die in Christ. It is not "preaching someone into heaven" to acknowledge his or her faith and the works that have been the fruit of that life. The minister is free to say of those who die in faith that for them, to live was Christ and to die was gain.

The closing prayer or benediction follows the funeral sermon or remarks. With this prayer, led by the minister or another, the service concludes. The minister's great hope and prayer is that the funeral has functioned as an instrument of healing in the hearts of all who were present. The ministry to the grieving is not over, but the funeral has established an emotional landmark for the family and the church.

Funeral Customs and Rituals

Every funeral service happens in a cultural context. Funeral customs arise from the traditions of the church and the community. Ministers must become familiar with funeral customs in their particular locations. Conversations with church members and with the local funeral directors can provide a good, early understanding of the rites and rituals expected. Working through a few funerals in a particular area will reveal the more subtle aspects of local funeral services.

Most of my ministry has been in West Texas and Central Texas, though during earlier years we served for a while in Las Vegas, Nevada, and in New Mexico. The framework provided here grows largely from my Texas ministries. Readers should not accept these forms as normative but welcome the challenge to make note of these customs and expectations and compare them to those in their home settings.

Acts of Kindness

When the word goes out that death has come to a family, Christian brothers and sisters go into action bringing food to the family and offering to help make the house as ready as possible for the arrival of the family and friends. Some of the dearest people I have known are the ones who went to the home of a freshly bereaved family and began washing the dishes, changing the sheets, and mowing the grass. One woman I knew had a standard package of plastic cups and plates, disposable dinnerware, napkins, paper towels, toilet paper, and tissues that she brought to every bereaved family. Often, after the funeral was over and the family reflected on the way people had responded to their loss, that package of disposables was seen as a key to caring for the influx of people into the home. Ministers do well to support and encourage the creative and loving folks who act in such kind and generous ways.

In all the churches I have served over the past forty-five years, the women of the church, sometimes with the help of a few good men, planned and presented a meal for the family before or after the funeral itself. Customs vary among congregations and cities. In smaller churches, often the entire meal is homemade. In others, a main dish is purchased from a local restaurant or caterer and enhanced with homemade sides and desserts. In every case, the minister was expected to be present and usually expected to welcome the family and bless the food. This meal expressed the love of the church for the family and offered the minister an extraordinary opportunity to interact with the family. I have always appreciated having these meals before the funeral service because I have always heard a story about or quote from the deceased that added to what I intended to say in the service. Ministers should know and encourage the members who provide these meals. They are precious servants.

The Visitation
A custom that has taken hold broadly over the past ten years is the visitation at the funeral home, usually on the day before the

funeral. The custom incorporates some of the aspects of a wake or a Catholic vigil. Often, the family brings framed photographs or family albums. The funeral home may produce a video or slide show. Sometimes, simple refreshments are served, other times just coffee and water. Ministers should drop by the visitation, though usually they have no specific responsibilities at this event. However, the visitation does give ministers the opportunity to express their personal sorrow to family and friends without performing some professional or ministerial function.

Funerals in the Church or Funeral Home

Ministers are usually responsible for coordinating the order and participants of the funeral, whether it occurs in the church sanctuary or in the funeral home chapel. They do not have to do everything, but they are expected to make sure the funeral runs smoothly. Ministers make sure that all other speakers know when they are to speak, what they are to say, and how much time they are allotted. They work with the worship leader, music minister, or those who will provide special music to make sure those details are in order.

As the start time for the funeral approaches, the minister or the funeral director will gather all the family together to arrange them for their entrance into the chapel. Typically, the widow or widower of the deceased enters first, accompanied and supported by a son, daughter, or other close relative, followed by the other children, grandchildren, siblings, nieces and nephews, and other relatives or close friends who have been included in the family circle. Even though the tradition has been that the one closest to the deceased enters first, I have found that the widow, widower, or other closest relative does not need to sit on the end of the pew next to the aisle. This individual needs people on both sides, offering support. For example, for the funeral of a man survived by his wife and grown children, I would have one of the children, with spouse if present, lead out to sit on the end seat. This allows the widow to sit surrounded and supported by her family.

Usually, after the order of entrance is arranged and before the family enters, the minister offers a prayer of blessing on the family and those gathered for the funeral. Then the minister will lead the family into the chapel to be seated on the first several rows with the audience. Typically, a staff member from the funeral home is present to assist in directing family who need to begin the next row. Upon entering the chapel, the minister goes directly to the podium or stage and motions for the audience to stand as the family enters and is seated. The minister and any other participants who are to sit on the stage go to their assigned place and stand until the family is seated. Then the minister directs all to be seated and the funeral proceeds. If the funeral home chapel has an anteroom for family seating, the minister may still enter the chapel and motion for the audience to stand while the family enters, even though most in the audience cannot see the family.

After the funeral service, the minister has a customary place that varies depending on whether the casket is open or closed when the service concludes. If no casket is present, the minister often has the audience stand as the family is ushered out of the chapel. If the casket is present but remains closed, the minister has the audience stand and then walks ahead of the casket as it is taken out; the family walks behind the casket, usually in the same order they entered.

If the casket is open and the audience is allowed to pass by to pay respects, the minister has the audience remain seated and then moves to stand at the head of the casket. The funeral director usually moves from row to row, indicating when the guests should rise and move toward the casket. The minister remains at the head of the casket until the entire audience has passed by.

The last people remaining in the chapel will be the family and the close friends. They will pass by the casket in inverse order of their closeness to the deceased. The minister will be there to console, hold, and steady those who pass. Those few last people who pass by will linger to say some last good-byes. This is holy ground. The minister is not expected to hurry people along.

When the casket is moved, the minister walks just ahead of the casket as it is taken out of the chapel. The minister will always be at the head of the casket whenever it is moved. When the casket is moved from the hearse to the grave, the minister walks ahead. When the casket is placed on the stand over the grave, the minister stands at the head of the casket and makes all graveside remarks from that position.

Itemized Agenda for the Funeral:
The Script, the Players, and the Moving Parts

A funeral is a holy event, but it is an event with a beginning, ending, and multiple players and moving parts in between. Writing down the details in an itemized agenda for all the participants will help assure that things go smoothly. This is just a sample agenda of a simple service in a church. A full agenda might include details or instructions that are essential to an orderly progression:

Order of Service

1:45 Family will gather in the anteroom (or a classroom or extra chapel). Minister leads a prayer of blessing over the family before they enter.

2:00 Participants enter and are seated on the stage. Family enters while praise team sings or other music plays. (Agenda should include order in which family members are lined up.) After family is seated, praise team sings or other music is played.

2:05 Presiding minister welcomes attendees.

2:07 Presiding minister or family friend presents summary of the obituary.

2:10 Music
List musical numbers or hymns and indicate if they are to be sung by the congregation or presented as special music. If audience will use hymnals, include numbers.

2:18 Family friend leads prayer.

2:23 Tributes (no more than three):
On behalf of the family
From a community leader or childhood friend or close coworker or colleague

2:33 Presiding minister gives the eulogy.

2:40 Prayer

2:45 Praise team sings (or musicians play) as the family leaves the sanctuary. Family will go directly to the cars (or to a reception area).

2:50 Funeral director may direct attendees to exit a row at a time past the casket, or one of those who participated in the service may give directions to the audience about directions to the cemetery or where they may greet the family.

Graveside Services

The graveside service serves many purposes. This service may be the only funeral there is, with only the family present or with others invited. A graveside service usually follows a chapel funeral service. In more cases recently, a more private graveside service precedes the larger chapel memorial service. The graveside service has at least three possible variations: the pre- or post-chapel funeral service, the stand-alone service, and the graveside service that is conducted in a different city from the funeral service.

The graveside service that is connected to a funeral service needs to be simple and brief. The family and friends have just sat through or are about to sit through a longer and emotionally charged hour. The graveside service should reflect the minister's consideration of the family's emotional load. The graveside service has four basic parts: a welcome, a brief word from the minister, a reading of Scripture, and a closing prayer. My personal guideline is to restrict my remarks to five to ten minutes—maximum. A few of the right words honoring the deceased and the family combined with a reminder of hope in Jesus is enough. If the deceased is a husband or wife of a long-standing marriage and if the mate is there, I always acknowledge the honorable completion of the "until death parts us" vow.

Sometimes the family invites someone to speak or read at the graveside who does not have a role in the larger funeral. A song might be played or sung at the graveside that might not have been deemed right for the funeral service. That doggerel poem written by a relative might be better read at the graveside than in the larger service. You may learn that the deceased is the member of some order of folks who have a graveside ritual. A minister may feel inner resistance to some lodge getting the last word at a Christian's funeral. Just let it go. The graveside is not the place for dealing with that kind of question. Let the Masons or whomever do their thing.

At the end of the service in our part of the country, the minister and the pallbearers, if there are any, remove their lapel flowers, place them on the casket, and shake hands with those seated on the front row of the gathering. At some country funerals, female members of the family may have a rose or other flower to lay on the casket as well. In Austin, Texas, the funeral director concludes the service, not the minister, and gives a thinly veiled commercial. I do not like ending the service this way because the service should remain focused on honoring the life of the deceased rather than the business of dying. Austin is the only place I have seen this done.

The stand-alone graveside service does everything that the family wants done at a single time and place. The graveside-only service may be chosen because of financial considerations, because the deceased directed the family to have only a graveside service, or because the family believes only a few will be able to come to the service. The graveside-only service is also the most common service for the death of a baby late in a pregnancy or as a newborn.

The basic format of the graveside-only service is very similar to the regular funeral, only compacted. If the family had wanted a full-blown funeral service, it would have chosen one. The minister thwarts the intent of the family if he or she plans an hour-long service. A graveside-only service should be no more than twenty minutes because many will be standing.

The service begins with a welcome and reading of the obituary, a message of consolation and hope, reading of Scripture, and a closing prayer. The family might want a song or a person or two to give a word of tribute—but limit it to only one or two if at all possible. One of the worst things that can happen at a graveside is for someone to open the service for anyone to share a story or experience—always an awkward disaster that can go on and on.

Very hot, very cold, or very stormy weather can and should shorten the service. I did a graveside service in Cross Cut, Texas, with the temperature at 12 degrees and the wind chill at minus 4. It lasted about three minutes. The living were in pain and eager to get back to the warmth of their idling cars.

The graveside-only service is not less important than a more complex funeral. The life of the deceased is not less important just because less ceremony is involved. The minister is the one most responsible for keeping the significance of the deceased in everyone's sight.

The graveside service conducted in a different city from where the funeral service occurred is much like the graveside-only service. Most of the family and some of the people who were present at the chapel funeral will be present at the graveside in the different city. This internment site probably has been chosen because it's the location of a family plot, it's where the deceased lived, or it's where the deceased one's family lives. A good number of those in attendance at this graveside were not at the chapel service. This service has a welcome and reading of the obituary, words of hope and consolation, Scripture reading, and a closing prayer. In addition, the minister can share highlights of the chapel service. Brief reviews of the words of tribute offered there may be meaningful to this new audience. Also, being in the old home area may mean that the family would want to have someone who could not be in the chapel service participate in some way. The minister needs to be flexible with such requests. Rarely should this type of service be longer than twenty minutes.

When a Flag Drapes the Casket

At the graveside service, and during a chapel funeral, a veteran's casket may be flag-draped. If a military honor guard has been assigned, the playing of "Taps" and the presentation of the flag to a family member will conclude the service. Sometimes, if no honor guard is present, the funeral attendants will fold the flag and present it to the family. Occasionally, the minister is asked to give the flag to the family member and does so with the words, "On behalf of the president of the United States and a grateful nation, I give you this flag. Thank you."

If the burial is at a veterans cemetery, the cemetery director will inform the family or funeral director of any special rules or customs that must be observed. If an honor guard will be firing a salute, it's helpful and less startling to the family if they've been told ahead of time at what point that will happen. Veterans cemeteries usually enforce very tight time limitations on services at the graveside or in their other facilities.

When the Casket Is Very Small

The graveside service for an infant is heartbreaking from the start. The minister has probably been with this family for days. Gallons of tears and volumes of "what-ifs" will have come and gone by the time the funeral service takes place. Still, the finality of the loss, the shockingly small size of the casket, and the tides of emotion that sweep through those gathered make this one of the most difficult moments in a minister's life.

This service will not be long. The themes are "We are here because of a great loss," "We are here with questions we can barely ask, much less answer," "We wonder where God is, but we trust that his heart has broken with ours." This is the time for sharing psalms of lament like Psalm 22. I have used the words David spoke after the death of his son in 2 Samuel 12:23, "I will go to him, but he will not return to me."

The minister is free to see this child as one known and loved by God, attended by angels, and now in the presence of the Father. Matthew 18:10 says, "See that you do not despise one of these little ones. For I tell you that their angels in heaven always see the face of my Father in heaven." Resist trying to explain what God is doing in allowing this death to occur. No one knows all that. This funeral service will end with much of life still broken. The minister is more faithful leaving it broken than pretending to fix it. This service ends with prayer, tears, and hugs, and for the minister, a great ache. I remember stumbling in tears across the Babyland section of an Abilene cemetery after the service for Ian Perry, the newborn son of dear friends. A part of my heart remains there, stumbling and weeping across Babyland.

No book, no length of service in ministry can prepare a minister for every type of funeral he may be called upon to preach. For example, I have never had to do the funeral for a child between a few days old and sixteen years old. I have minister friends who have lived with children through cancer journeys. I have preacher friends who have had their own child die. I have been blessed, out of hundreds of funerals, never to have had to deal with the death of a child or adolescent. Still, I have thought myself through various tragic circumstances that would end a child's life: accidents, sicknesses, sudden deaths, long illnesses.

This gives a minister the opportunity to imagine what the right things to say and do might be when a particular kind of death, dying, and grief situation comes up. I have found it to be of great value to imagine my way through the deaths of those who are near death or to put myself in a death scene I have not actually experienced. I have thought through hospital scenes. I have imagined myself sitting with broken parents and friends. I have thought about funeral structure and the emotional price to be paid to walk through such a deep shadow of life. I am not a somber, inward person, but I don't think it is wise to assume nothing so terrible will ever happen. We might as well think through our responses, so we will be better prepared if or when the phone rings.

Payment to Ministers for Funerals

The traditional position of ministers with regard to pay for weddings and funerals is that ministers do not charge for them. They are a part of ministry. Still, it is appropriate and common for families to express their thanks in some monetary way. If, however, a minister works hours with a family and concludes a complicated funeral and graveside service and there is no check, that just has to be fine with the minister. I can say that over the years, people have been more than kind in their honoraria. To be sure, the minister may appropriately expect the family to cover expenses if the family asks her to travel very far to do a funeral.

Customs surrounding funerals vary from place to place. Each minister should consult with the church and with the local funeral directors to get a clear understanding of funeral expectations in a particular place. Performing these functions in a confident, calm way creates an environment of peace around the family that honors and protects them. Visitors from outside the faith will leave the service with a more positive impression of the church and the faith if the service is handled in the way most appropriate for the community.

Serving the Unchurched with the Love of Jesus

Occasionally, a minister is privileged to minister to unchurched people and their families during some stage of the dying process or when they need assistance with a funeral service. "Unchurched" here is intended to designate someone who has enough faith in God to seek spiritual companionship during dark times, but not enough personal commitment to Jesus to be active in the body of the church. Usually, the minister does not get the call to serve truly godless people at these times. But frankly, as death approaches, fewer people fit that description.

Sometimes these opportunities are presented by church members who ask the minister to help members of their family or neighbors who are not practicing their faith. Another source may be local funeral directors. In most communities, the minister should offer her or his services to the local funeral directors, helping with funerals when families do not have a church connection but want a minister to do the funeral. These opportunities are great blessings if the minister is able to receive them as such.

Being a Minister to the Whole Community

When I was twenty-four years old, I served as a volunteer police chaplain in Albuquerque, New Mexico. I delivered death notifications, ministered to survivors at accident and crime scenes, and counseled people who were at odds. Not one of the people I dealt with as a chaplain was a member of my church. I learned that the opportunity to be salt and light in the world is a great privilege that calls out of you every gift you have and some you didn't know you had. I learned that being a minister in service to unchurched people puts you in circumstances that Jesus would understand, like the time I was called to tell the mistress of a murdered man that his wife had shot him. Ministers challenge their church members to be Jesus to those around them. I want to challenge ministers to be Jesus to the community around them by finding ways to minister to the community outside the church in times of loss and grief.

The experience of working with funeral directors as clergy on call began during my ministry in Trent, Texas, at age twenty and has given me some of the most poignant moments of my ministry. In Carlsbad, New Mexico, the funeral director called and asked if I would do a funeral service for a sixteen-year-old boy who had been riding in the passenger seat of one of two cars that were drag racing on a public street. The car he was in was winning. He leaned out the window to taunt the following car and fell out the window into the path of the trailing car. Foolish. The funeral was an opportunity to speak to dozens of teenagers about life and choices and to minister comfort to several families of young men who were involved in various ways. It was awful to be sure, but it was exactly where the light of the kingdom most needed to shine that day in southeastern New Mexico. You hope that being there will create a moment of clarity for the young people in the room that might someday save their life. But you don't know, and it's still the right place to be.

My encouragement to ministers is to be brave, to be vulnerable, to be available. The minister has significant contributions to make to the dying and grieving while life remains and to the family and friends at the funeral.

Being Jesus to Others

The stages of denial, anger, bargaining, depression, and acceptance are the way most people deal with bad news, not just the faithful. For this reason, the minister offers great mercy and compassion when he or she joins a person who is dying without saving faith and Christian hope. The dying person may have never experienced someone who could be fearless in the face of death and dying. For the dying person, the listening ear, gentle questions, and thoughtful observations of the minister may well be as close to the person of Jesus as the person has ever come. The one dying may decide to come to Jesus in those last days.

The minister also serves the family as it works through its tension because of the different stages of grief its members are in or because of unresolved conflicts that the stress of their loved one's dying is bringing to light. In this context, the minister listens for the questions and comments that might lead to sharing more about Jesus. These verses from 1 Peter encourage thoughtful interactions with unbelievers, so that those outside of Christ might be impressed by the love and grace of the Christian response to life and ask for more information about this Lord who creates such life:

> Conduct yourselves honorably among the Gentiles, so
> that, though they malign you as evildoers, they may see

your honorable deeds and glorify God when he comes
to judge. (1 Pet. 2:12 NRSV)

Do not fear what they fear, and do not be intimidated,
but in your hearts sanctify Christ as Lord. Always be
ready to make your defense to anyone who demands
from you an accounting for the hope that is in you;
yet do it with gentleness and reverence. (1 Pet. 3:14b–
16a NRSV)

These opportunities to meet people on the ground of grief and loss
are incarnational moments. The minister empties herself or himself and enters the world of these wounded, unchurched people
with love and without judgment. The minister drops any professional, ministerial distance and meets the family and friends on
level ground. The minister is not called to be God's word of con-
demning judgment but to be God's latest word of mercy and grace.
This is the time to pray for just the right words and actions at just
the right time. Pray for wisdom, and then act as if God has given it.

Interacting with unchurched families will allow the minister
to know what spiritual resources the members of the family have.
Very rarely does a family have no religious background at all. Most
people know some bits of Scripture. Most know Psalm 23, the
Lord's Prayer, and maybe John 3:16—though they may not know
what a 3:16 is. People will tell stories of going to church when they
were children. They may have memories of some sweet church
people. They will tell stories of horrible, usually judgmental things
that happened in a church—things that made them leave, vowing
never to return. The minister is not obligated to defend the ugly
things that some church or church member might have said or
done in the past. The minister is obligated to hear and hurt and
pray and stay.

Funerals for the Unchurched

The opportunity to accompany an unchurched family on its grief journey before death is somewhat rare. More often, the minister receives a call from a local funeral director asking if the minister can do a funeral for an unchurched family. The funeral of the unchurched shares many of the elements of the funeral for the faithful described in Chapter Five, but a few alterations are necessary.

The minister will meet with the family of the deceased. This initial conversation will establish the depth of any faith in the deceased and in the grieving family. This conversation or some other visit before the funeral will give the family an opportunity to talk about the deceased one's life. The minister always hopes there is something in these conversations that gives some grist for the funeral remarks.

On one occasion, I met with the family about the funeral for the father. I asked if he had passed on any wisdom or wise sayings. "No." I asked if there was any religious background. "No." I asked if there was anything about him that stood out. After a long silence, "Well, he liked to bowl."

I thought, "A man lives his whole life, is married, has a family, has a career, and the only thing those closest to him can say about the residual impact of his life is 'Well, he liked to bowl.' Amazing! Sad. And now I have to do a funeral with just this?" I was pretty sure I would not have to do much to exceed the expectations of this family. It was very sad, but I couldn't say that—God loves all.

Most often, families will share stories and words of wisdom passed on from the deceased that will help frame the text of the funeral. In these early conversations, the minister will become very aware of the absence of faith language and hope or of the presence of hopeful assumptions about the eternal outcome of the deceased's life. Many unchurched have basically a universalist view of the outcome of human life, assuming that living and being some sort of nice person leads to eternal life. During all these conversations, the minister remains aware that this deceased person has passed into the presence of the loving God, who will do what is right with those who die.

The funeral of the unchurched has a certain structure that is much like the funeral for the faithful. The service needs to be planned to last no more than an hour. The minister will welcome all to the service and lead a prayer. The minister or a family member or friend will share the obituary, and as always the obituary is better if it is told rather than read, with a few stories added out of the experience of the one sharing the obituary.

The tributes will come from friends and family. The music and the tributes in a funeral for the unchurched may be very different from what one expects at a churched person's funeral. Not too long ago, a woman asked me to speak at the funeral service for her son who had drunk his way through his liver by his late twenties. This was an awful, tragic, unnecessarily early death. The music at the funeral was raucous. The friends who brought tribute shared memories of drinking bouts and included stories from a party honoring the deceased at a bar the night before the funeral. The culture that contributed to the death offered its own sotted tribute at the funeral. The irony was palpable. Then I spoke about how precious his life was in the sight of God. I talked about how much his parents had loved him and had fought for his life through the years. I talked about how God knew his heart and how he wrestled with his inner darkness and weakness. I talked about how his early death was tragic and was a cautionary tale for others. His was not a path to be followed. I reminded the audience that he was in the hands of our loving God who would do what was right.

The structure and content of the funeral sermon allow words of truth, comfort, and life. The minister tells the truth: "This death has come too soon." "This loss is so tragic, beyond words." My third funeral after entering full-time ministry was for an unchurched man in Trent, Texas. He had taken his twenty-year-old grand-daughter dove hunting for the first time. In the course of the hunt, she tracked a dove too far to the left and shot her grandfather in the head. The beginning of that funeral was a true word about the tragic circumstances. In another instance, a woman from our church had an unchurched, alcoholic, plumber father. He was funny. He was always a bit out of bounds. I began the funeral with, "John Doe, he was just a mess." We all laughed together, and the funeral proceeded.

The minister spends some time in the remarks sharing the virtues of the deceased's life, the way the family has loved him or her, and memories the family has shared during what were prob-ably brief meetings. Reflect on the ways this person's life was a gift to those around, then end this section of the funeral sermon with some form of the true word that the deceased has passed into the presence of the loving God who will do what is right.

The funeral sermon for the unchurched then has a pivot that moves the focus of the remarks from the memory of the deceased to a challenge for the living. This word to the living has this form:

- Today, we are sure that life is precious and death is real.
- Today, we are reminded that God has loved us and through his Son Jesus Christ has provided a path to eter-nal life, blessing us here and in the life to come.
- Today, we can reflect on our own lives and the path we are taking, because we too will pass into the presence of the God who loves us and who will do what is right.

I have used this sermon structure on many occasions, and no one has been offended by the gentle presentation of the good news that is in Jesus. Stories are out there of ministers preaching hellfire-and-damnation sermons at funerals. Personally, I cannot imagine anything more unlike what Jesus would do in a family's moment of sorrow. Tell people of the love of God in Christ in as attractive a way as possible in the context of the funeral.

At the graveside service for the unchurched, welcome all, read Psalm 23, offer a few closing words and a closing prayer. Remarks reminding all that we have come from dust and return to dust are appropriate. In the closing remarks or prayer, again say that the deceased has passed into the presence of the loving God who will do what is right. That will be the second or third time that phrase has been said, but it is a truth that must be embossed on the service.

Ministry to the unchurched during times of death and grief offers the minister an extraordinary opportunity to pour the love of Christ into a family. Conducting these funeral services in a good and appropriate way will enhance the reputation of the church in the community. Working through such difficult situations will bring the minister greater spiritual maturity. When the funeral director calls about a funeral for an unchurched person, answer the call.

8

Obituaries as Ministry and History

By Cheryl Mann Bacon

When someone died in our church family, my mother was always the first one to show up with a cake or a casserole. I write obituaries.

For most of us, an obituary is the last thing written about our lives. For some, it's the first. Thus, if the funeral sermon documents the theology of one's life, the obituary documents the history. As a result, I've always considered it an honor when a family accepts my offer to write the story of their loved one's life, if only in brief.

Obituaries are not eulogy. The purpose of an obituary is not to laud the character of the person or to wax eloquent and sentimental about her finest characteristics and how sorely she'll be missed. An obituary tells the history of a person's life by providing the most important facts. That said, a well-written obituary is neither cold nor formulaic. Obituaries are truthful, accurate, complete. Life is interesting. The events of life make up its whole.

A news story may tell about the event of death. An obituary tells the story of a life.

Writing the obituary should not be a task for the minister, whose service to the family and preparation for the funeral already demands significant preparation and emotional energy. Occasionally, if a person has endured a long decline, the preparations made in advance of death may include having someone draft the obituary, or at least gather the pertinent facts to aid in its preparation. Some individuals may even have written their own. But more often, it's a task left to an already overwhelmed family member who made As in English, or who didn't.

The Business of Obituaries

Some funeral homes will prepare an obituary, typically from a standard template, and most take responsibility for placing it in the local newspaper or other newspapers the family requests. Too often, families have no idea they are committing to pay hundreds, even thousands of dollars for these services and publications.

For a church member with talent and experience as a writer, perhaps a journalist or English teacher, writing an obituary is ministry, and a minister who can recruit such a collaborator is fortunate. An experienced writer who understands concision and craft will be able to include the historical details that should be included, the personal details that matter most to the family, and do so in a cost-effective fashion when that is important.

What most people in the United States refer to as obituaries are actually purchased classified advertisements. They are not cheap. A few major newspapers, such as *The Dallas Morning News*, charge by the inch. More commonly, obituaries, or "in memoriam announcements" as they are sometimes called, are priced per line. A small town daily may charge less than a dollar per line; major regional papers a few dollars per line. The *Los Angeles Times'* charges begin with $105 for a one-inch, five-line announcement; and on the opposite coast, the *New York Times'* announcement of nineteen lines run for three days is more than $1,400.

As with other forms of advertising, the cost increases based on the newspaper's circulation size, whether or not a photo is included, how many and on which days of the week the obituary is published, and other factors. Some newspapers do run "death announcements" or "funeral announcements" at no charge, typically limited to two to four lines and submitted by local funeral homes. Because of liability issues, most newspapers will not accept announcements from family members unless they are verified by the funeral home.

Funeral homes and newspapers often have relationships with online obituary websites such as Legacy.com that include guest books and other features. A funeral home may post to one of these sites at no additional charge or a newspaper may include its own online posting and guest book for free or at an additional cost.

Major newspapers and some smaller ones regularly include obituaries that were written by journalists about prominent members of the community, or about individuals whose lives were not well known but are particularly interesting, or whose passing is particularly poignant. These are not news stories about death, but narratives about life. The best ones take a "warts and all" approach, sometimes wry, sometimes seasoned with humor or pathos, always committed to factual commentary. The best are brief biographies, though some stretch to two thousand to three thousand words or more. The obituary pages of the *New York Times, Washington Post,* and the *Los Angeles Times* are masterfully crafted and make fascinating reading. But they include only a tiny handful of those whose deaths are recorded on the printed or digital page.

The obituary may also be printed in the program for the funeral service that is prepared by the funeral home for a fee or by the church. For families who cannot or choose not to pay for an extensive obituary in a large local newspaper, the printed program presents an opportunity for a longer obituary that provides a keepsake for family and friends. The obituary writer who welcomes the opportunity of telling the fuller narrative of a person's life can provide the longer version.

How to Write an Obituary

The first time I ever contacted a family in order to write an obituary, I was a twentysomething public relations writer working for a university. I don't recall the student's name, only that he had been killed in a traffic accident while away from the campus in the summer. I didn't know him or anyone in the family and still recall the knot in the pit of my stomach as I dialed the father's number. I was fearful of offending him, of intruding, of invading his grief. The conversation taught me a great lesson. People want to talk about their loved one. Even though I was but a stranger's voice on the line, that grieving father was anxious to tell me all about his son, and he wanted to be sure that anyone who read my story would know the truth about his life. It provided some brief inoculation against his greatest fear—that his son's short life would be forgotten.

In gathering information for the obituary, a face-to-face interview is always preferable to a phone call, and is best if it takes place in the home of the deceased where photos and remnants of life provide details that may be omitted by human sources whose memories are stressed by grief.

Part of the challenge of the conversation is that it needs to happen very soon after the death so that the obituary can be prepared, checked, approved, and submitted to the funeral home and/or local newspaper by a deadline that is typically early afternoon on the day before publication and may be earlier for Sunday editions. As a practical matter, this means that if a person dies on Monday and a funeral is planned for Friday, the obituary needs to run by Thursday at the latest. To meet a Wednesday afternoon deadline, the writer needs to interview the family no later than Tuesday. Even a fairly brief obituary of 400–500 words can require several hours of research and writing.

Without significant personal knowledge or a thorough and well-organized file of information, the only way to gather all the needed facts is to interview at least one person who was close to the deceased. While a crowd of family members can be distracting, having an extra person or two nearby who may recall names, dates, and details can be helpful.

Having a plan for the interview is important. Australian scholar Nigel Starck writes about obituaries, obituarists, and their history. He describes two basic forms of the genre: the snapshot and the portrait. Virtually all obituaries published as paid advertisements fall into the snapshot category. In *Life after Death: The Art of the Obituary*, he suggests a standard but typically British formula.[1]

Starck's bias, one often shared by journalists and professional obituarists, is that the snapshots in paid obituaries are generally colorless or, worse, they are filled with overwritten purple prose by well-intended family members. The list and examples provided here are Americanized and designed to show that even a snapshot can be personal yet professional. Often, this can be accomplished by weaving two or more categories of information into a single sentence or brief paragraph.

Full name and nickname if relevant. Remember, this is history. Don't leave readers and historians wondering what Buddy's real name was.

Date and place of birth, place in birth order, where the person grew up.

Parents' names. This paragraph covers birth order, parents' names, early years and education, and provides some insight into personality and background:

> J. C. was the third child and only son of J. C. "Joe" Sr., and Kate Jackson Mann. He was reared in Fort Worth and told "Cow Town" stories to anyone who would listen. He walked a paper route during the Depression while his father ran a switch engine in the Santa Fe rail yard. He attended Paschal High School until his father sent him to Abilene to finish his senior year in high school at the Demonstration School, later named Abilene Christian High School, graduating in 1937.

Another example includes these same facts and sets the scene for a life that was a classic rags-to-riches story:

> Varner was born in a tent in Ranger, Texas, on Dec. 20, 1919, to George Virgil Varner and Christina Shafer Varner. His father and grandfather were contractors providing mules to haul oil field equipment during the Ranger oil boom.

Education and other professional certifications, college degrees. Typically, this just means listing the degrees and sometimes field of study, but it is also an opportunity to include interesting facts that describe the person:

> After her older children were grown, she returned to the college classroom, taking advantage of the three free semester hours she received each semester as a faculty spouse. She earned her college degree from ACU in 1983 at age 62 after 13 years of course work, graduating the same year as her youngest son, Robert; she was selected as a speaker for the Senior Luncheon.
>
> Mary Jo also took an ornithology course at Sam Houston State University one summer while Norris was a visiting professor, which continued a lifelong interest in birds. She kept a lifetime bird list and made a special trip to see the Texas bald eagles.

Career, including employer and years in employment. Some of the dates for events in this example were provided elsewhere, but the facts in this single paragraph sum up the uniqueness of the woman's career progression:

> Dr. Durrington's service as an educator and academic leader included elementary school classrooms, the principal's office, the AISD boardroom, university faculty and administrative roles, and statewide appointments. Friends and colleagues have known Colleen in these leadership roles for so long that many have forgotten she came to such tasks later in life than most, having married at 18 and raised a family before she ever completed her bachelor's degree. Once she returned to school, she became a teacher, principal, professor, chair and dean in rapid succession.

Military service, if appropriate, including rank, decorations, theatres of conflict. For those who served in peacetime, the list may be fairly perfunctory, but for those with active duty in war or conflicts, some aspects of the person's life may be well demonstrated by this history:

> In 1943, he joined the U.S. Army as a chaplain with the rank of first lieutenant, attending the Army Chaplains School at Harvard University. During his three years in the Army he was awarded the European Theatre of Operations ribbons with campaign stars for Normandy, Northern France, the Rhineland, the Ardennes and Central Europe. He also was awarded the Bronze Star medal with two oak leaf clusters. In 1946, he was discharged with the rank of major. Although he always referred to his service under Patton as "just a remote member of his command," he was interviewed in 1971 by the *Dallas Times-Herald* about his memories of Patton's famous address to his troops that was reenacted in the opening to the motion picture *Patton*, and described it in detail.

Accomplishments and awards; membership in professional, civic, or volunteer organizations and offices held. These should be grouped, and if the list is very long, use only the most significant or long-held.

Marriage(s), when and to whom. Family may prefer to omit previous marriages that ended in divorce, but they do have historic relevance, particularly if children were produced by the marriage:

> She married David Jones on Jan. 17, 1967, and they were married for 19 years and had two children. After moving

to Albuquerque, she met Greg Cox, a local realtor, and
the two married July 16, 1990.

Children, including names and location. Often this can be woven into the narrative.

Places of residence throughout life. These details are important but almost always can be worked into other paragraphs.

Date, place, and cause of death. Families may choose to omit the cause of death, but traditionally it's included for historical reference. Hospitals often have lobbied local newspapers or funeral homes not to state the name of the hospital where a person dies, thus the frequent use of "at a local hospital," or "at a local care facility."

Survivors. The surviving spouse, children, and number of grandchildren comprise the minimal list of survivors. Commonly, if space allows, names of children's spouses and names of the grandchildren are included. If the obituary is to be published in the hometowns of the children, their place of residence should be added:

> Smith is survived by her husband, James, of Dallas,
> and three children: Bill and wife Sadie of Midlothian,
> Caryl Johnston and husband Dylan of Silver Springs,
> Maryland, and Alan of Frankfurt, Germany. She is
> also survived by three grandchildren: Hannah Smith,
> Ramsey Johnston and Karen Smith.

Funeral arrangements, including burial or interment. If burial is private, make that clear.

Family preferences for memorial gifts. This question should be part of the interview with families. Some families have an immediate response, and others have not considered it at all and require some time to make an appropriate decision. The phrase "in lieu of flowers" that often precedes the list is largely superfluous. Those who wish to send flowers will do so and may also be among those who make memorial gifts. The obituary should not deny permission to those whose generosity and condolence will be expressed in either manner.

The exact order in which these facts are shared varies slightly according to regional preferences and their relative importance in the person's life. As a practical matter, readers are looking for information about the service, so placing that in the first or second paragraph is helpful, but it may also be included near the end. Survivors and memorial gift preferences are always last.

While the family is typically the first source from which to acquire this information, experienced obituary writers always fact-check. Objective, authoritative sources and documents from employers, newspaper clippings, professional associations, and universities can be very helpful. More than once, a family has told me about a deceased person's degree and field of study that did not match university records.

I follow Associated Press style, and my strong bias is to take a journalistic approach, both in conveying the facts of a person's life and in crafting description and narrative that tells its story. This type of obituary runs without a byline, so once I hand it over to the family or funeral home, I accept their edits without objection, so long as they don't include actual falsehoods. The family is purchasing the space and has final say in what is included or excluded.

Note

[1]Nigel Starck, *Life after Death: The Art of the Obituary* (Melbourne: Melbourne University Press, 2006).

When Death Is News

By Cheryl Mann Bacon

"A time to be born and a time to die."

When the writer of Ecclesiastes wrote about the seasons of life, he began with these. Some may argue about the universality of at least a few of the other couplets. For some, there may never be a time to kill or a time to uproot. But to each of us is given a time to die.

For most of us, that time will pass unnoticed by the world except for those closest to us; but when a confluence of unusual tragedy, crime, prominence, or human interest converge, death may become the focus of local or even national news. Few families and ministers are prepared for the challenge of death in the public eye.

News coverage about death is not a new or inappropriate phenomenon. Coverage of death by newspapers in the United States predates the American Revolution and has continued—through some eras in grisly detail and through others with sentimentality and moralizing. Over time, and particularly since the late twentieth century, this coverage has increased in importance and prominence. The focus of most such coverage inevitably is on the living, on ties to the past, on cultural lessons for the future.

Scholars have concluded that, in addition to conveying facts, such coverage creates a shared mourning, and in times of shared disaster can create a feeling of consensus.[1]

Most deaths lack the scope of impact that would garner attention from the news media. But when television reporters gather in the front yard of a recent murder victim, or when the death of a longtime community leader prompts the local newspaper to do a retrospective on the person's life, those in ministry should be prepared to support the family of the deceased in their interactions with journalists and to model Christian character by treating those media representatives with respect.

Because for most families and ministers, the challenge of facing the media in a time of tragedy is rare, few have really thought much about it until confronted with it. For journalists, however, covering tragedy is a common occurrence, and so professional organizations have spent significant time and research creating guidelines and codes of ethics for their members. Some individuals may conjecture that "it's against the law" to cover funerals, but the courts have been clear that any event that is open to the public can legally be covered by media. In actuality, most news organizations take far less license in covering tragedy than the law allows.

Ethics and Guidelines Followed by Journalists Covering Deaths

One of the four principles of the code of ethics of the Society of Professional Journalists (SPJ) is to minimize harm, detailing the importance of balancing what is legal with what is ethical, showing compassion for those affected and recognizing that "private people have a greater right to control information about themselves than public figures and others who seek power, influence or attention."[2]

The Radio Television Digital News Association (RTDNA) offers specific guidelines to its members about covering funerals that begin with the words:

> When journalists cover funerals, they must do so with
> the highest degree of sensitivity and professionalism.
> Although stories of funerals can be deeply moving,
> newsworthy and even healing for an audience, there is
> great potential for journalists to intrude on a family's
> privacy and cause pain to already vulnerable people.[3]

One of the most important questions journalists and ministers must consider is whether the family welcomes coverage of a funeral or other events. Some prefer privacy. Others want the story of their loved one to be told. As this book was being written, its primary author was deeply involved in conducting the funeral of a highly esteemed former chief justice of the Texas Supreme Court who died at age 103. Media coverage included major newspapers across the state and professional legal publications, all of which was appropriate in light of his prominence and influence.

Dear friends of mine, a family whose ten-year-old son died after a two-year battle against brain cancer, welcomed coverage of their son's treatment, events held in his honor, and ultimately the funeral because they wanted his life and their faith to serve a greater purpose and example.

Not every family is prepared for such coverage, however, and the minister's role may be to help family members think through what they are comfortable with and what requests for privacy they wish to make. Even when circumstances of the death have been widely covered, few news organizations will expect to conduct photo or video coverage of a funeral or burial unless they are invited, and then the RTDNA guidelines encourage them to let viewers know they were invited.

Death by suicide presents particularly sensitive issues for media. Comprehensive guidelines for covering suicide were published in 2015, developed by a group of organizations focusing on suicide prevention, public policy, and mental illness, in collaboration with schools of journalism, media organizations, and Internet safety organizations. Extensive research has shown that "certain types of news coverage can increase the likelihood of suicide in vulnerable individuals." The guidelines may also be helpful to ministers as they consider how to talk about a suicide in public or written form.[4]

Why Is This News?

News coverage of a funeral and of a death itself are very different. The same SPJ code of ethics that encourages sensitivity and restraint in covering funerals also requires journalists to "seek truth and report it." The minister who understands why the death of someone in the church or community has attracted attention from local or even national media is in a better position to support the family and, at times, to be a spokesperson for the family or the church. A good starting place is understanding what makes something newsworthy. Journalists are trained from their first newswriting course about what makes an event newsworthy, but the public is not always as aware of these criteria:

- Timeliness: Is this new information? Has it just happened?
- Prominence: Is the person or persons involved in this story well known?

- Proximity: Did this event happen nearby? Are people in this community affected?
- Impact: Are a large number of people affected?
- Human Interest: Does the story have an emotional element that touches all of us? Is it interesting because of concerns or achievements we have in common?
- Conflict: Are opposing forces in play? These forces may present themselves as a conflict between powerful people or organizations, conflict between value systems, structured conflicts such as an election or sporting event, even the conflict of man vs. nature.

When several criteria are at play in a death, the likelihood of media attention increases. So, for example, when the longtime mayor, business leader, or local sports hero dies, the criteria of prominence, proximity, and number of people affected come into play. If the person was controversial, then conflict may also be a factor. If the prominence was regional or national in nature, then the coverage will be also.

When a tornado wipes out an entire neighborhood, leaving several people dead, every criterion is present. Perhaps the victims were not prominent, but leaders will comment and be called on to address the situation. Natural or man-made disasters always generate human interest stories: a soldier survives multiple deployments only to die in a flood; a small child survives a hurricane that killed every other member of her family; a firefighter dies saving others.

When violence takes the life of a local teenager, or a freak accident or auto collision kills innocent bystanders, or a member of the armed services is killed in action, all of these criteria may come into play.

This is not a bad thing. Media coverage at such times can help create a place of communal mourning and understanding.

> Journalists have the power to attribute meanings to the events, to dramatize the event as out of ordinary—as something that speaks about symbolic values—and to select the emphasis by focusing on specific acts and specific actors that mould the social experience of ritual.[5]

The reach of this public mourning has only been extended by the pervasive cloak of social media. We may wince at the prospect of selfies at funerals and other invasions from the ether, but as social platforms are engaged by an increasingly broad demographic, they become part of the fabric of conversation and community. The minister or communications minister may be in charge of communicating with church members using email or social media. This should happen as soon as possible after the family has been notified. While it may be desirable to ask members to wait twenty-four hours or until extended family members have been notified before posting to their own social media, in reality, once those outside the immediate family learn the news, any notification control is lost. Friends and relatives will begin posting tribute statements and words of sympathy to family members, even posthumous messages on the deceased's Facebook page or via Twitter.

Two rules of crisis management are well applied here: If it's bad news, make it old news fast; and, tell it first and tell it yourself. Your best chance to control the content and tenor of a message is to be the first one to share it.

Responding to Media Inquiries

The circumstances, public interest, and prominence of individuals involved may result in media coverage leading up to or immediately following the time of death. When a minister understands what has made a death newsworthy, she can better anticipate the attention and help the family anticipate questions.

Today, many large churches have a communications minister with training in media relations. Others have crisis response teams that include a designated media spokesperson. Such resources can be helpful. Usually, the church is a less likely point of contact for the media than family, but the minister may be contacted and asked to be an intermediary with the family to determine if they are willing to be interviewed or would welcome media coverage. Occasionally, the minister may serve as a family spokesperson; but more typically, that role is left to a family member. Thus, the role of the minister or communications minister may be to help the family designate a spokesperson, prepare statements, remind them to keep track of contacts with the media, and protect the privacy of the family members who are least prepared to face the media.

The family spokesperson does not have to be a member of the immediate family. For example, if a child has been killed in a random act of violence, an aunt or uncle may be a good spokesperson. Few parents have the emotional strength at such a time to speak on camera, though they may want to be interviewed; people want to talk about their loved one. The spokesperson needs to be knowledgeable about the deceased, the circumstances, and plans. He or she should be comfortable fielding questions in front of cameras and disciplined enough to stay on message. The spokesperson must be sincere, believable, and authoritative but nonconfrontational.

When possible, connect with public relations professionals at the deceased person's employer who may be better prepared to handle inquiries. They may have a complete biographical file and may even have a person who is willing to be the media contact. If you are fortunate enough to have a public relations professional who is a member of your church, seek her advice and involvement.

Cultivate Good Relationships with the Media

Journalists have a job to do and may be more uncomfortable with the questions they must ask than the family member is in answering them. Usually, family will be dealing with local media, people who live in the same community and probably have great empathy for this tragedy and its impact on the community as a whole. Don't beg. Don't intimidate. Try to make it easier for them to do their job well.

Be Available

Keep the names and numbers or email addresses of every journalist who contacts the family. Make every effort to return phone calls or reply to emails within thirty minutes, even if only to say, "We won't know any more until tomorrow afternoon. You're welcome to call then," or something similar.

Be Truthful

Don't be evasive. *Never say, "No comment."* If you can't answer a question, say, "I'm sorry, I can't answer that." If you don't know, say, "I don't know." If you can answer a question tomorrow but not today, say that. If you've been told to refer certain questions to law enforcement or legal counsel or some other authority, say that. Just don't say, "No comment." It inherently implies that you're hiding something.

Don't Go off the Record

Don't say, "I'll tell you, but you can't use this." Doing so can create an ethical and professional dilemma for the journalist when a competitor gets the same information from some other source.

Don't ask to be an anonymous source. Once you have shared information with a reporter, he is entitled to use it—it's not fair to go back after the fact and ask him not to do so.

Become Familiar with Media Needs and Deadlines

Most reporters will post information to social media or to the news organization's website immediately, but they may have other deadlines for specific newscasts or publication. It's always fine to ask, "What's your deadline?"

Be Prepared

If the spokesperson has agreed to a press conference or to appear at some other entity's press conference, compile a list of questions in advance that might be asked, formulate answers, and help him practice. Use the STARCC method that is widely used in times of crisis by public relations professionals in healthcare circles.[6] Craft statements and responses to questions that are

- Simple—People don't want to hear big words.
- Timely—People want information NOW.
- Accurate—In an emotionally charged situation, people won't get nuances, so give it straight.
- Relevant—Answer questions in practical terms.
- Credible—Empathy and openness are keys to credibility.
- Consistent—The slightest change in the message is upsetting and will be dissected by all.

In other chapters, we have seen how ministry to the dying and the family of the dying includes "a time to weep and a time to laugh, a time to mourn and a time to dance." When confronted with a death whose circumstances warrant the interest of news media and a broader community, the instinct to withdraw and embrace "a time to be silent" may be overwhelming. Welcoming instead "a time to speak" and speaking that truth clearly and kindly better serves the interests of the family and the one they mourn.

Notes

[1]Carolyn Kitch and Janice Hume, *Journalism in a Culture of Grief* (New York: Taylor & Francis Group, 2008), xii.

[2]"SPJ Code of Ethics," revised September 6, 2014, at SPJ's National Convention in Nashville, TN. https://www.spj.org/ethicscode.asp.

[3]"Guidelines for Covering Funerals," created by Al Tompkins, The Poynter Institute, for Radio Television Digital News Association's Journalism Ethics Project, 2014, http://rtnda.org/content/guidelines_for_covering_funerals/index.html.

[4]"Recommendations for Reporting on Suicide," American Foundation for Suicide Prevention; Annenberg Public Policy Center; Columbia University Department of Psychiatry; National Alliance on Mental Illness, New Hampshire; Substance Abuse and Mental Health Services Administration; Suicide Awareness Voices of Education, 2015, http://reportingonsuicide.org/.

[5]Mervi Pantti and Johanna Sumiala, "Till Death Do Us Join: Media, Mourning Rituals and the Sacred Centre of the Society," *Media Culture & Society* 31, no. 1 (January 2009): 123.

[6]Department of Homeland Security, *Pandemic Influenza Preparedness, Response, and Recovery: Guide for Critical Infrastructure and Key Resources*, Sept. 19, 2006, 78, https://www.dhs.gov/sites/default/files/publications/cikrpandemicinfluenzaguide.pdf.

Through the Shadows to the Light: Extended Pastoral Ministry to the Grieving

As I write this, seven months have passed since my mother died.

Five months have passed since my father died.

Time rolls on, leaving the matters of grief and loss to be worked out as best we can. To be sure, my parents lived into rich old age and died when it was time. I am not beset with overwhelming grief. Still, I do need to remember them in a proper way. I need to hold them in a respected place in my heart. From day to day, I could use a little companionship along the way. This experience of my own reminds me of the way that my ministry to the grieving should unfurl for their benefit and wholeness.

As ministers and pastors, we commit to the spiritual care of those in our flock. For those in our circle of loving responsibility, we have the opportunity to have a longitudinal ministry of compassion, helping people gather up their grief into healthy inner markers and monuments of memory. I want to suggest how we can do this in a good way.

Matching Stride with the Grieving

Whether you are walking with a family in your church or near you in some other way through a death, the journey is long, and it's meant to be that way. When our ministry to the one dying is done, we are often left with the family and close friends who are affected by the loss. The level of the residual grief will be somewhere on a spectrum from mild and intermittent to intense and constant. This grief, in some form, will last a long time.

I think that "walking with" expresses well what we do as we accompany people in grief. You have noticed, no doubt, that when you actually walk with someone, the two of you fall into matching strides. You don't have to think about it. It is just what people do. Our response to the grief of others is not so autonomic. Left to ourselves, we may avoid or resist rhythms of the grieving gait, tempted to speed along or slow it down. But as ministers, we are called to stride intentionally into the lives of sorrowing folks and match our response to their grief to the place of their grief. We may be surprised at times at how long the journey is. Eugene Peterson titled his book *A Long Obedience in the Same Direction* on the Psalms of Ascent (Psalms 13–134) in light of an observation by the German philosopher Friedrich Nietzsche: "The essential thing in heaven and earth," Nietzsche noted, "is . . . that there should be long obedience in the same direction." In the same way, we must be able to sustain our focus on those recovering in grief.

Not all ministers are gifted for this kind of ministry. We have to respect those who are called to ministries of evangelism and other short-term interactions with people. However, in every church, some ministers and members need the gifts of someone who knows that life doesn't resolve situations into tidy conclusions over a weekend or in forty days of prayer.

The Story of a Long Abiding

A few years into my ministry with University Church of Christ in Abilene, Texas, one of my elders, who was the husband of our bookkeeper in the church office, had a heart attack midway through a weekday afternoon. The call came into the office. Soon, Wanda, his wife, and I were walking into the hospital. John was gone. Wanda was left with two children and her church family. The sudden death of a great, godly man began a companionship in grief that continues even today.

We made it through the funeral in that numb way that you do when you suddenly lose someone close to you. We said good things; we sang the right songs. Desolation and the painful journey with grief came anyway. Since we were together in the office or in church six days a week, we had the opportunity to walk along together. Some days, silence was the proper, respectful thing. No one has the strength to dig deeply into her own psyche every day. My place was to walk into her office most days and say, "Hi." It was her choice as to what to do with my open door to further conversation. My job was to be completely open to however she might be feeling. She was and is a magnificent lady, so all her feelings, questions, and affirmations came out of a mature, stable, faithful heart. We shared her fears for her children. We shared her aching, lonely feelings. As we turned through the calendar, we got to the one-year mark. She told me at that point, "They say that after a year, your grief should be easing. That is not true." Her candor helped me—after a year, grief is not done. And so we continued as fellow travelers on the road of life as it is. Now we have been a brother and sister joined in grief for thirty-four years. I saw Wanda again in the summer of 2017, more than thirty years after John's death. The message passed eye to eye and in our hug gave testimony to the pain, the healing, and the joy we have shared.

The journey I've just described is precious to give as a gift. The thoughtful minister will be on this kind of journey with dozens of people at the same time, and the minister needs different tools to do it well.

The first and most important tool you bring to your ministry is your own self, being transformed by the continuing work of God—Father, Son, and Spirit. This is a constant in all of ministry, but ministry in the presence of death and loss will reveal shallow hearts and uncertain faith. As I have written earlier, we must be in the process of dealing with our own mortality and, by extension, with the losses we have experienced among our own family and friends. We don't have to be finished with all our personal griefs to minister to the grieving. We do need to be moving along a healing path. We can't be stuck in an unhealthy place with our losses.

With our own hearts set for ministry, we are ready to use the tools of compassion: presence, persistence, remembrance, stories, songs, and wisdom. You will think of other tools that you have in your ministry toolbox. May God bless you as you use them.

Presence

A person grieving loss can go through times of isolation. Friends can withdraw, especially if the friend group is made up of couples and death has taken a spouse. Friends can withdraw because they don't know what to do with their own grief. They may think that showing up in the life of the bereaved will bring more pain to the bereaved. They are not really avoiding the discomfort of the grief by withdrawing, but their own discomfort.

Ministers give the gift of presence. Their presence is calm and nonjudgmental. Ministers know how to be with someone and be quiet. Ministers know how to listen. Ministers are not repelled by anger or sorrow. Ministers offer their time to the bereaved without expecting that the gift of time will suddenly fix the brokenhearted or restore shattered dreams. Ministers are willing to be present with what is.

The willingness to be present comes out of an awareness in the minister that simple presence is a very powerful tool, or even medicine, in caring for those in grief. At the point that some loved one has been taken, it may seem that God and others have withdrawn. Showing up as a minister is a part of God showing up.

Persistence

Persistence makes presence powerful. Showing up once or twice in order to get the information necessary for a funeral only satisfies the minimum requirements of ministerial duty. The real test of the minister is what happens in the weeks and months to come. Persistent grief ministry grows out of the minister's ability to be faithful to a task. This faithfulness is not faithfulness to doctrine but commitment to a task. The steadfast love of the Lord never fails. Because of this, God is called a faithful God. He fulfills his promises. He stands by his people. We minister to others with the same standard of trustworthy performance.

No one will get grief ministry 100 percent right every day, but we should try to keep our focus on the wounded among us. We make it a point to speak to them when we are together at church. Just a word can make a difference. Just a "How are you? How are things this week?" can lighten someone's load. A card, brief note, phone call, or email can serve as a reminder that a loss is not forgotten. For a long time, I had a system that would prompt me to send out cards to those recently bereaved at one month, three months, six months, and a year after the death had occurred. Having a calendar with those prompts loaded in it is very important. The fact that you have a system for reminding you to do something that you want to do does not make it less meaningful. Really, the very fact that you intend to be persistent in this aspect of ministry is a credit to your heart. Out of such faithfulness, the beatitude promise is fulfilled: "Blessed are those who mourn, for they shall be comforted."

Remembrance

Ministers use the ways they remember the deceased to continue the healing process in those who have experienced the loss. Saying that you remember something that their loved one did or said is such a sweet gift to give someone who has experienced loss. Sharing such remembrances, whether brief or extended, is thoughtful and kind.

An example of this is the story that my collaborating author's father would come to my office and tell me at least every year that he attended University Church of Christ in Abilene. J. C. would come in, asking for a few minutes. Then he would tell me about his being in the U.S. Navy before and during World War II. He had a story about being in battle, standing on the deck beside a friend. An enemy shell hit the ship near him and his friend suddenly disappeared. The suddenness of the loss and the fact of his own survival never left his thoughts.

He was so aware of the gift he had in his life. The visit with me always ended with his story of the most meaningful church service in his life. He had been at sea for a long time. The ship docked in Ceylon on Christmas Eve. J. C. got to go ashore. As he walked around the town, he heard the Christmas music coming from a missionary Methodist church down the street. The instruments were filling the air with sweetness, inviting him in. He was not a Methodist, but that night it didn't matter. He needed to be in worship. He needed the fellowship of Christmas joy. J. C. always came to tell me this story when someone had indicated in some way that our Church of Christ tribe was God's only people. He didn't believe it. He had heard the music of a broader fellowship in the air of Ceylon.

Though several years have passed since J. C. 's death, this story will ring true for Cheryl when she reads it. This story will be one I can tell her through the years to communicate that I remember her father. These are the kinds of stories that ministers need to remember and share as opportunities present themselves.

The other side of remembrance is what stories the bereaved remember of the one they have lost. The wise minister will often ask questions that give folks the opportunity to tell a meaningful story. Sometimes, these stories are ones that allow the bereaved to retell the circumstances of the death to be able to work through how things happened or how they acted in the time of crisis. Other stories highlight meaningful moments in which the life of the storyteller was touched in some significant way by the deceased.

One story that I heard several times was from D. C. Cox. He would tell me how his wife Bethel died. The Coxes had a ranch south of Abilene. One fall day, they decided to take a drive across the ranch to get out and see the land they loved. As they were driving across the grassland prairie, D. C. noticed that the hot catalytic converter on the pickup had left a trail of fire behind them. The fire was exploding behind them in the persistent West Texas wind. D. C. drove away from the fire, but they found themselves boxed in, pinned between the fire and the barbwire fence. All they could do was try to run for it. They got out of the pickup and ran, as well as eighty-year-olds could, running toward the fence to get over it to safety. Bethel couldn't get over the fence. D. C. said he struggled to help her get over the fence. She couldn't do it. He stood at the fence, frantically working to help her as the fire burned into the fence line. The fire was burning D. C.'s hands and arms as it engulfed

Bethel. D. C. watched the fire take his wife of decades. And he would say at the end: "There was nothing I could do."

He told me that story several times over the years before he died. He needed to tell the story, I think, so I would affirm his final words. He needed me to say, "D. C., you are right. You did all you could. I am so sorry. That was so hard. It was awful." He didn't need to be declared innocent. He always regretted that they took the drive across the grassland. He needed to tell the story and have someone take his burn-scarred hands and love him in his grief.

Most often, people tell stories to highlight the wonderful ways the departed one blessed their lives. In Abilene, in the shadow of Abilene Christian University, I heard a recurring story from several families through the years. It was the story of the young mother who was suddenly widowed and had to find a way to care for her family. This story of the heroic, young, widowed mother always touches me.

The story would begin with a love story. A young man and young woman would have found each other, usually in some way connected with college or military life. The couple married and had a time of sweet beginnings—new home, new job, new home church, and then children. To be sure, these stories had an idyllic lens over those early years, but that was forgivable because of the darkness of tragedy that soon settled over it. The husband died. Sometimes it was illness; sometimes it was accident. Whichever it was, the end result was a woman left alone with children to raise.

For these women, the solution to the questions about how they would support themselves and how they would raise their children was that they would move to Abilene, Texas. The mother would get a job at Abilene Christian University (Abilene Christian College then), and the children would go to the campus school. The little family would live in a little house near the campus. Mother would take a job and become an invaluable part of the exceptional staff of people making the college function. They would go to church at University Church of Christ. The family life was held, nurtured, and insulated in the Abilene Christian University enclave.

These stories were usually told by sons and daughters who wanted to ensure that their mother's character and sacrifice were not forgotten. They had twin statements: "Our mother made us everything we are," and, "Women like my mother made ACU what it is today."

Because people have stories like this to tell, the minister helps the grieving process by prompting them to tell their stories. The thoughtful and observant minister will ask questions:

"How did you meet your husband/wife?"

"Tell me about when he proposed."

"Where was the first place you lived?"

"When is your anniversary? What is your favorite memory from an anniversary?"

"What kind of mom/dad was she/he?"

"That's a beautiful ring. Tell me about when he/she gave it to you."

These questions are more tender, and you have to be more thoughtful when asking a parent about their lost children . . . but this is still the way forward for those in sorrow:

"Tell me about the day he/she was born."

"What was his favorite story?"

"What was the funniest thing he/she ever said to you?"

"Who were his/her best friends?"

Any observation you can make or question you can ask that leads a person to tell a story about the one they have loved and lost helps them move along the road of grief toward settled, healthy memories.

Songs and Wisdom

A special set of questions I have found to be very helpful involve mining out memories of favorite songs and words of wisdom. Music finds its way deeply into our relationships. Our faith and our church songs grow intertwined in us. When planning a funeral, we always ask about the most appropriate music for the funeral service, because music moves people. It conjures up memories and moments and voices. We need to remember that memories about music will continue to be a text for remembering and recovering.

The minister will want to ask:

"What was 'your' song?"

"What were the songs in your wedding?"

"What song at church makes you remember him most?"

Even, "Is there a song that you kinda wish we wouldn't sing in church when you are there?"

Words of wisdom are also significant in grieving memories. I always ask, "Did your dad have favorite Bible verses, wise sayings, or advice that he gave you at important times in your life?" You hear the heart of the one who died in the remembered words:

"You can do all things through Christ who gives you strength."

"You are here for a purpose. Don't rest until you find it."

"When better than now? Who better than you?"

"Don't be afraid."

Hope for the future lies in the wisdom, even the humor, of the deceased.

The journey with someone going through grief can be long. How do you know when you are doing well and making progress? It is good when a person can sit through a worship service without bursting into tears and fleeing the room. But, I have found that the real marker is sweet and simple in a way. When those in grief begin to celebrate the birthday of the deceased more than they find despair on the anniversary of the death, they've made progress.

I had a dear friend who would tell me about going to the grave of her husband. I knew my grief work with her was about done when she started going to the gravesite on her husband's birthday instead of on the date that he died.

So our ministerial task in the presence of death and grief binds us to a long, attentive journey. We may need some administrative help to do it well. We would be smart to have a file on each family needing our attention, so we can make notes of stories we have heard and told, of songs and proverbs shared, of prayers and Scriptures offered for comfort. All of the help will be good. What we need most is our own prepared heart with as much of the fruit of the Spirit poured into it as we can open ourselves to receive.

The Church of Sorrows and Acquainted with Grief

The work of ministry in the lives of the dying and those who love them cannot be accomplished if only professional clergy are willing to welcome such a heavy challenge. The church as the body of Christ in the world must be able to respond appropriately to all the turns life can take. This challenges churches that want to build their image on just the sunny side of life. The gospel of health and wealth has little to say to those deep in sorrow and walking in the deepening shadow of their own deaths. Traditions that overemphasize evangelism, the Second Coming of Jesus, recovery from addictions, and other aspects of ministry may miss their opportunities to serve those in sorrow. To be sure, Scripture has much to say about our bodies, our money, the lost, the Second Coming, and victory over sin in all the ways it comes, but the church needs to seek balance in its attention to all the phases of the human condition, including ministry to those dealing with grief, dying, and death.

Balancing a church's view of ministry and life begins with faith that God is at work in all things to work his will in the world. Not everything is good, but God intends to redeem every moment and circumstance. God enlisted the natural world in the process of working all things from the devastation of the Fall into the glory of the redemption of all things in Christ. Paul writes of the comprehensive work of God in the created order:

> I consider that our present sufferings are not worth comparing with the glory that will be revealed in us. For the creation waits in eager expectation for the children of God to be revealed. For the creation was subjected to frustration, not by its own choice, but by the will of the one who subjected it, in hope that the creation itself will be liberated from its bondage to decay and brought into the freedom and glory of the children of God.
>
> We know that the whole creation has been groaning as in the pains of childbirth right up to the present time. Not only so, but we ourselves, who have the firstfruits of the Spirit, groan inwardly as we wait eagerly for our adoption to sonship, the redemption of our bodies. For in this hope we were saved. But hope that is seen is no hope at all. Who hopes for what they already have? But if we hope for what we do not yet have, we wait for it patiently. (Rom. 8:18–25)

In that work of creation pushing, urging us toward the refuge of God's adoption, we experience a spectrum of events and emotions. We are arrested by the beauty of a sunrise. We are threatened as hurricanes and tornados spin out destruction, injury, and death. We are comforted at our blood tests. We are decimated by a CAT scan. At such times, we seem to be victims of a natural caprice; but ultimately, we are in a natural world put in service of higher powers.

This section in Romans 8 is followed by the assurance in verse 26 that the Spirit within the Christian is at work to help in times of weakness, and in verse 28 that God is at work in all things "for the good of those who love him, who have been called according to his purpose." The Spirit would not need to be on duty in us to help us with weakness if we were not challenged by weakness, within us and without. God would not need to be at work in all things if he had made the world to always tilt in our direction.

The challenges listed in the "more than conquerors" section in verses 35–39 are exactly the situations in which God works his glorious, beneficent power: trouble, hardship, persecution, famine, nakedness, danger, sword, life, death, angels, demons, the present, the future, powers seen and unseen. Danger lurks in all the bad things that can happen. Temptation lurks in the shadows of all the good things that can happen. The church that can stand in love, compassion, and service when death is stalking its beloved ones is a church that believes that God comfortably works his glory in a world that is full of awful things.

How a church that constantly confesses Jesus can forget that weakness, pain, bewilderment, suffering, reproach, and death often come before deliverance, resurrection, and restoration is beyond me. Good news manufactured without the cross is a lie. The church that cares for people in the difficult times of life, in the shadows of grief and death, is a church that has a rich theology of the cross and Easter.

The worship of the church must reflect this balanced, clear-eyed, faithful relationship with life as it is and God as he is. The worship in a church sold on health and wealth will have a certain canon of Scripture and playlist of songs for worship; it will overemphasize praise, victory, and the certainty of deliverance right now from every heartache and hangnail, and it will distort the church. When a church sees sadness as a sign of faithlessness and a threat to its character, that church has left the real world and moved to Disney World.

Learning Lament

The Psalms provide the emotional atlas of the church. They remind us that faithful people have raised their voices to God in many different ways. Interspersed with the psalms praising God for mighty works, calling the faithful to holiness, thanking God for calling his people into being are the psalms of lament. These darker psalms ask why and how long. In them, the church understands God's willingness to hear our grief, questions, and complaints. Psalm 22 is the most quoted psalm in the New Testament. It begins:

> My God, my God, why have you forsaken me?
> > Why are you so far from saving me,
> > so far from my cries of anguish?
> My God, I cry out by day, but you do not answer,
> > by night, but I find no rest. (Ps. 22:1–2)

Hear the faithful one calling out to God who seems absent and inattentive? Of course we hear. We heard these words from Jesus on the cross. Lament is the sound of the suffering faithful. God can leave us wondering when he will deliver us, wondering if he will at all.

> Restore us again, God our Savior,
> > and put away your displeasure toward us.
> Will you be angry with us forever?
> > Will you prolong your anger through
> > all generations?
> Will you not revive us again,
> > that your people may rejoice in you? (Ps. 85:4–6)

In Psalm 90:13, the psalm attributed to Moses, we hear a cry for God to relent in mercy: "Relent, LORD! How long will it be? Have compassion on your servants."

Certainly the children of Israel raised their voices with questions and complaints as they shuffled across the wilderness. The psalmist here gives voice to the heartache and emptiness of God's people in a difficult place.

Now, no church should become a Lament Church, only full of dirge and moaning. That would be a distortion as great as the Health and Wealth Church. Still, most churches have an underdeveloped vocabulary of lament and a heart reluctant to express the raw emotion and questions inherent in lament. Because of this inadequacy, churches and individuals are often tongue-tied in the presence of grief and loss. In that crucial moment, just when they most need to join in the pain of a person or family, or just when they most need to give voice to a loss felt churchwide, just then the church with no aptitude or vocabulary for lament will have nothing to say. And the hollow silence will reverberate.

Immediately after September 11, 2001, our churches needed worship of lament. In other times of significant loss in fire, flood, tornado, hurricane, or other natural disasters, churches need to be able to express in lament the pain and bewilderment of the faithful before God. The Psalms, Lamentations, the lament found in the prophets should be read. The church sings the Redmans' familiar lyrics: "You give and take away. You give and take away. . . ." Because of our confident faith in God, we are able to express strong questions and bitter objection to the perceived state of things.

Individual members of the church need to be able to enter into private conversations of lament and prayers of lament. We must be able to pray for deliverance *from* difficulty. We must be able to pray for deliverance *through* difficulty. We must be able to pray out the language of lament with hurting people *in* difficulty. Only the church that can respond to the hard things of life with deep, intentional lament has the right to articulate hope and move on to praise. Psalm 22, beginning with, "My God, my God, why have you forsaken me," moves through a range of authentic expressions of dark emotion. But having expressed all that clearly, it ends with these words:

> All the rich of the earth will feast and worship;
>> all who go down to the dust will kneel before him—
>> those who cannot keep themselves alive.
> Posterity will serve him;
>> future generations will be told about the LORD.
> They will proclaim his righteousness,
>> declaring to a people yet unborn:
>> He has done it! (Ps. 22:29–31)

Gifted to Serve

The church that ministers well to those in grief, loss, and dying has a sound foundational theology and a rich vocabulary of worship. Such a church also recognizes those among its members who are spiritually gifted to minister to those with death-related burdens. Some quickening of the Spirit led Joseph of Arimathea to think of offering to care for the body of Jesus. Joseph, with Nicodemus, bought spices and received the devastated body of the Savior. They embraced the responsibility of showing up and following through in a very difficult situation. Nothing about the body of Jesus on Friday pointed to any Sunday resurrection.

The women who went to the garden on Sunday morning were working out of the same internal imperative. The men had done the best they could in laying Jesus to rest. The women probably knew it could be done better. They were undaunted by the early hour, the likelihood of Roman guards, the ugliness of death, the shock of early decay. They remind me of the widows who had taken dead Dorcas and washed her body and laid her in her bed, awaiting Peter's visit. Blessed are they who are settled enough with their own mortality and their own sense of the gifts God has given them that they can be with death and sorrow in all its forms and with the people who have been touched by such loss.

These good folks from the Gospels and Acts had something in them that drew them to the place of death. Their desire to step in to help was stronger than their desire to run away, protect themselves, and escape from the gritty ugliness of death. Their need to give action to their grief made them excellent servants and ministers in the time of death and loss. Our churches today have people exactly like this.

The church needs to be aware of the giftedness of its members. Who are the brave and tenderhearted? These gifted people do much good when they flow into the lives of those who have just learned of their advanced disease, as they move to help families where death has come, to have conversations with those who are dying, to continue to care for those who have months and even years of grieving to do. They need to be quietly honored for and called to this service.

Because this kind of ministry requires so much emotional and spiritual energy, the leadership of the church must attend to the spiritual health and well-being of its ad hoc grief ministers. This can be done by offering words of thanks. It can be done by offering talented, gifted people access to additional training in grief ministry. These folks are treasures in the life of the church.

Over forty-six years of ministry, I have at times been blessed to minister in churches unafraid of sorrows and acquainted with grief. Such a church has a clear understanding that the cross preceded the resurrection. This church will have a capacity to rejoice and praise God. This church will also have a mature capacity to speak and worship in the vernacular of lament. This church will know and value its ministering servants who are gifted with abilities to enter the house of sorrow and death with the love of Jesus. May we all seek to bring this maturity to our churches, our worship, and our ministry.